THE PIP

ANTHOLOGY OF WORLD POETRY OF THE 20TH CENTURY

VOLUME 4

Edited with a Note by
Douglas Messerli

EL-E-PHANT 4

GREEN INTEGER
KØBENHAVN & LOS ANGELES
2003

GREEN INTEGER BOOKS
Edited by Per Bregne
København/Los Angeles

Distributed in the United States by Consortium Book
Sales and Distribution, 1045 Westgate Drive, Suite 90
Saint Paul, Minnesota 55114-1065

(323) 857-1115/http://www.greeninteger.com

Design: Per Bregne
Cover: [left to right, top to bottom]
Miguel Hernández (drawing by Antonio Buero Vallejo); Gyula Illyés
(photograph by Layle Silbert); Else Lasker-Schüler (drawing by
Paul Lasker-Schüler); Octavio Paz (photograph by G. Giovanetti/Effigie/Bilderberg),
Vítězslav Nezval (photograph by Foto Czech News Agency);
Andrée Chedid (courtesy of the author); Luis Cernuda (drawing by
Ramón Gaya); Nelly Sachs (Stockholm Riwkin); Oliverio Girondo
(drawing by Carlos Alonso)
Typography: Kim Silva

LIBRARY OF CONGRESS CATALOGING IN PUBLICATION DATA
Messerli, Douglas ed. [1947]
The PIP Anthology of World Poetry
of the 20th Century
Volume 4
p. cm — Green Integer / EL-E-PHANT 4
ISBN: 1-892295-87-3 (alk. paper)
I. Title II. Series

Printed in the United States of America on acid-free paper.
Green Integer books are published for Douglas Messerli

THE PIP ANTHOLOGY OF WORLD POETRY
OF THE 20TH CENTURY
VOLUME 4

GREEN INTEGER
6022 Wilshire Boulevard, Suite 200A
Los Angeles, California 90036

(323) 857-1115 fax: (323) 857-0143
E-Mail: lilycat@sbcglobal.net
visit our web-site: www.greeninteger.com

TABLE OF CONTENTS

A NOTE

In this, the fourth volume of my ongoing series of the *PIP (Project for Innovative Poetry) Anthologies of World Poetry*, I have again chosen basically from random, balancing a wide selection of modernist figures from many countries. I now see the whole series as encompassing at least fifty volumes. Only two factors will determine whether or not I can achieve this idealistic enterprise: finances and my death!

What has become increasingly apparent, in this horrible year of war, is the true need for such a series, the importance of helping English-language readers to know the writing and, by extension, the cultures of poets from around the world. In an interview with a Brazilian journal, I was recently asked to comment if I felt Americans, and by extension American poets, knew of the poetry in other countries. My conclusion was a bleak one: most Americans don't even know a poet in this country, I quipped; and, perhaps even more disturbing, is my guess that most American poets could name, perhaps, twenty poets from other countries. I recounted the story of a poet friend, very interested in international writing and who is engaged in reading the poetry of other cultures, innocently asking me who was the poet whose book I held in my hands. The book was the collected poetry of Léopold Sédar Senghor, the great Senegalese poet, former President of the Republic of Senegal, and one of the founders of the Negritude movement of French-speaking Caribbean and African writers who utterly transformed Francophone writing in the 20th century. My fear is that precisely this lack of knowledge of the writing and experiences of other cultures underlies the American arrogance and beliefs that not only is our culture superior to others, but that it should *be* the culture of others. It is no accident, I suspect, that a president who had traveled very little before taking office, could not comprehend that American values and methods of achieving those values were not shared by all others. I am not suggesting that poetry will change these conditions, but certainly it may help us to comprehend a world which—despite its astounding ability to quickly communicate—seems to be splintering apart rather than sharing ideas.

As always, a great many individuals have shared with me to produce this volume, most notably Gilbert Alter-Gilbert, Charles Bernstein, Jeanette Demeestère-Litman, Peggy Frankston, Pierre Joris, Martin McKinsey, Christopher Middleton, Murat Nemat-Nejat, Marjorie Perloff, Jerome Rothenberg, Hiroaki Sato, Milos Sovak, Paul Vangelisti and many others. The Young Research Library of the University of California, Los Angeles must again be thanked for sharing its resources. Diana Daves has devotedly overseen this book and the others in the series; Kim Silva has excellently resolved the typographical difficulties of this book; and Shana Feibel helped in the proofreading. All the many translators and publishers named within have made this volume possible, and should especially be commended. Finally, I must thank the international board of PIP advisors who, as friends and figures of international significance, have encouraged me to seek out and read over 1,000 poets from around the world.

—DOUGLAS MESSERLI

Vicente Aleixandre [Spain]
1898-1984

Born in Sevile in 1898, Aleixandre spent his early summers in Málaga, the place that spawned many of his later poems. In the early 1920s he moved to Madrid, participating in the discussions at the Residencia de Estudiantes, where many poets of his generation, including Federico García Lorca and Jorge Guillén, met and talked on a regular basis. But it was the poetry of Rubén Darío (see *PIP Anthology*, volume 1) that most influenced his early work, and stirred him to begin writing poetry as well.

His first poetry appeared in *Ambito* (Ambit) in 1928, after his friends had sent some of the works to José Ortega y Gasset's *Revista de Occidente*. Despite the obvious influences of other poets in these early poems, the work revealed many of the characteristics of Aleixandre's later writing.

Beginning in 1925, Aleixandre, having contracted tubercular nephritis, was secluded and had to curtail his activities. His second book, *Pasión de la tierra* (1935) (Earth Passion), is more clearly a result of his illness. Having recently read the works of Sigmund Freud and James Joyce, Aleixandre used various metaphors and similies through this work to present a sort of dialogue between eros and thanatos. Because of the Spanish Civil War, this important work, originally published in Mexico City, was virtually unkown in Spain until the mid-1940s.

In 1932 Aleixandre published *Espadas como labios*, written after *Pasión de la tierra*, but published previous to it. The book marked a return to versification and to a greater control of images. *La destrucción o el armor (Destruction or Love)*, also published in 1935, further explored erotic love against a background of a natural world which is in complete flux, alternating between destruction and transfiguration.

Written in 1934, *Mundo a solas* (World Alone) was published in 1950. This is a much darker and pessimistic book in its presentation of mankind's loss of primeval innocence.

During the Civil War, Aleixandre remained in Spain, where his home was nearly destroyed in the battle of Madrid. Accordingly, at a time when other poets immigrated or were murdered, he stood as an important figure of the great "Generation of 27." He was awarded the Nobel Prize for Literature in 1977.

BOOKS OF POETRY:

Ambito (Málaga: Litoral, 1928); *Espadas como labios* (Madrid: Espasa-Calpe, 1932); *Pasión de la tierra* (Mexico City: Fábula, 1935); *La destrucción o el amor* (Madrid: Signo, 1935); *Sombra del paraíso* (Madrid: Adán, 1944); *Mundo a solas 1934-1936* (Madrid: Clan, 1950); *Nacimiento últi-*

mo (Madrid: Insula, 1953); *Mis poemas mejores* (Madrid: Gredos, 1956); *Poesías completas* (Madrid: Aguilar, 1960); *Poemas amorosos* (Buenos Aires: Losada, 1960; enlarged, 1970); *En un vasto dominio* (Madrid: Revista de Occidente, 1962); *Presencias* (Barcelona: Seix Barral, 1965); *Retratos con nombre* (Barcelona: El Barda, 1965); *Dos vidas* (Málaga: El Guadalhorce, 1967); *Poemas de la consumación* (Barcelona: Plaza & Janés, 1968); *Obras completas* (Madrid: Aguilar, 1968; revised and elarged [2 volumes], 1978); *Sonido de la guerra* (Valencia: Cultura, 1972); *Diálogos del conocimiento* (Barcelona: Plaza & Janés, 1974); *Nuevos poemas varios* (Barcelona: Plaza & Janés, 1987)

ENGLISH LANGUAGE TRANSLATIONS:

Twenty Poems, trans. by Lewis Hyde and Robert Bly (Madison, Minnesota: Seventies Press, 1977); *Destruction or Love,* trans. by Stephen Kessler (Santa Cruz, California: Green Horse Three, 1977); *A Longing for the Light: Selected Poems,* trans. by Lewis Hyde and others, edited by Lewis Hyde (New York: Harper & Row, 1979; reprinted Port Townsend, Washington: Cooper Canyon Press, 1985); *The Crackling Sun,* trans. by Louis Bourne (Madrid: Española de Librería, 1981); *A Bird of Paper,* trans. by Willis Barnstone and David Garrison (Athens: Ohio University Press, 1982)

Closed

Bare earth. The defenseless
night alone. The wind
insinuates deaf throbbings
against it draperies.

The shadow of lead,
cold, wraps your breast
in its heavy silk, black,
closed. So the mass

is pressed down by the material
of night, famous, quiet,
over the limpid
late plain of night.

There are bankrupt stars.
Polished hinges. Ice
drifts along
in the heights. Slow streams of cold.

A shadow passing
over the mute grave contour
lashes, austere,
its secret whip.

Flagellation. Corals
of blood or light or fire
are divined under the gauze,
grow mottled, then give way.

Either flesh or the light of flesh,
deep. The wind lives
because it looks forward to gusts,
cross-currents, pauses, silences.

—Translated from the Spanish by W. S. Merwin

(from *Ambito,* 1928)

My Voice

I was born one summer night
between two pauses. Speak to me: I'm listening.
I was born. If you could only see what suffering
the moon displays without trying.
I was born. Your name was happiness.
A hope under the radiant light, a bird.
Arriving, arriving. The sea was a pulse,
the hollow of a hand, a warm medallion.
So now they're all possible: the lights, the caresses, the skin, the horizon,
talking with words that mean nothing,
that roll around like ears or seashells,
like an open lobe that dawns
(listen, listen) in the trampled light.

—Translated from the Spanish by Lewis Hyde

(from *Espadas como labios*, 1932)

The Bull

That lie or breed.
Come here, dogs, quick; fly away, dove; jump, bull,
bull made of moon or honey that won't come unstuck.
Here, quick; escape everyone, escape; I only want,
I only want to be at the edge of the struggle.

Oh you, most beautiful bull, a surprised skin,
a blind smoothness like an ocean moving toward its center,
a calm, a stroking, a bull, bull of a hundred powers,
facing a forest, stopped at the edge with horror.

Bull or world that doesn't,
that doesn't bellow. Silence;
this hour's so huge. A horn or a sumptuous sky;
black bull that endures the stroking, the silk, the hand.

Fragile softness over a sea skin,
hot and lustrous sea, sweet and powerful rump,
such wonderful abandon, the way this big thing lets
its almost cosmic powers flow down like the stars' milk.

Huge hand the covers up the sky-bull on earth.

—*Translated from the Spanish by Lewis Hyde*

(from *Espadas como labios*, 1932)

The Bottom of the Well
(The Buried Man)

There at the bottom of the well where the little flowers,
where the pretty daisies do not wave,
where there is no wind or scent of man,
where the sea never threatens,
there, there is that still silence
like a murmur muffled with a fist.

If a bee, if a flying bird,
if that mistake which is never expected
appears,
then the cold lasts;
the dream sank the earth straight down
and now the air is free.

Perhaps a voice, a hand now free,
an upward impulse wants to be moon,
or calm, or warmth, or that poison
of a pillow in the muffled mouth.

But sleeping is always so serene!
On the cold, on the ice, on the cheek's shadow,
on a lifeless word, already gone,
on the very earth, always virgin.

A board at the bottom, oh unnumbered well,
that illustrious smoothness which proves
that a shoulder is contact, is dry cold,
is dream always though the forehead be closed.

Clouds can now pass. No one knows.
That ringing…Do bells exist?
I remember that the color white or the forms,
I remember that the lips, yes, even spoke.

The weather was hot.—Light, consume me—.
It was then when the lightning bolt suddenly
would freeze in iron.
Time of sighs or of adore me,
when never the birds lost feathers.

Time of softness and permanence;
hoofbeats didn't pound in my chest,
the hooves didn't stay behind, they weren't wax.
Tears fell like kisses.
And in the ear the echo was already solid.

And so eternity was the minute.
Time only a huge hand
pausing over long hair.

Yes, in this deep silence or dampness,
beneath the seven layers of the blue sky I am blind to
the music jelled in sudden ice,
the throat that collapses on the eyes,
the intimate wave that is drowned on the lips.

Asleep like a cloth
I feel the grass grow, the soft green
that waits in vain to be curved.

A hand of steel on the grass,
a heart, a forgotten toy,
a coil, a file, a kiss, a piece of glass.

A metal flower that feels nothing
and sucks silence or memory from the earth.

—*Translated from the Spanish by Deborah Weinberger*

(from *Espadas como labios*, 1932)

Flying Fugue on a Horse

We've lied. Time a again we've always lied. When we fell backwards into an over-charge of light, into a fire of coarse wool slowed down with sleep. When we opened our eyes and asked what kind of a day it was. When we held her by the waist, and kissed that breast and, turning our head, worshipped the lead of the saddest after-noon. When for the first time we didn't remember the redness of her lips.

Everything's a lie. I myself am a lie, mounting the horse on a joker and swearing that my plume, this elegance that floats on my north winds, is a dryness that brightens my teeth, that polishes my gums. It's a lie that I love you. It's a lie that I hate you. It's a lie that I'm playing with a full deck and that the opening fan is forced to respect the color of my eyes.

What hunger for power! What hunger for running off at the mouth and for brute force slapping this afternoon's silent decline, which turns its palest cheek, as if fak-ing the death which is announcing itself, as if it were calling for a bedtime story! I don't want to! I'm not sleepy! I'm fed up with deafness and lights, with sad second accordions and wooden raptures that wipe out schoolteachers. I'm scared of getting stuck with my head hanging on my chest like a drop and that the sky's dryness will decapitate me for keeps. I'm scared of evaporating like a mattress of clouds, like a sidelong sneer that rips an earlobe. I'm in a panic that I might not be, that you'll slap me: "Hey you, Jack!" and I'll answer coughing, singing, pointing with my forefinger, my thumb, my pinkie, to the four horizons that don't touch me (but throw darts at me), that repeat me in the round.

I'm scared—listen, listen—that a woman, a shadow, a shovel, will gather me into her blackness, so velvety, so disarming, and will say: "I name you. I name you and I cre-ate you. I conquer you and toss you around." And raising her eyes, shipping me with her arms and a load of dirt, she'll leave me up there, stuck on the point of a smart-ass drill bit, which stings as it penetrates and eats away my eyes, loading all the sobs in my throat up on to my shoulders. That buzzing dazzling point that pierced the simplest blue so that innocent flesh remains exposed to the hooting of sheepskin hearts, those hardened smokers who don't know that blood drips just like smoke.

Ah, but it can't be! Horse of cups! Horse of swords! Horse of clubs! Let's get out of here! We'll climb the ladder of rags, that outdoor castle where the slowest caresses are sold at a loss, where our feet will be kissed and the tracks of the road rubbed out. Take me on your back, swords of the moment, card-bubble, misleading letter on the tabletop! Take me away! Wrap me up in the reddest cloak, in that flight of your tendons, and lead me into another kingdom, into the heroic ability to love, into the combination to every safe, into the wild dice you feel in your sad fingers when roses shipwreck next to the bridge of salvation. When there's nothing you can do.

If I die, leave me alone. Don't sing to me. Bury me wrapped in the deck I leave behind, in that lovely treasure that will know how to strum me like a sure hand. I'll sound like a fragrance from the depths, very grave. I'll rise to your ears, and from there, turned into pure vegetation, I'll debunk myself, untelling my own story, my own plot, flowing back into my mouth left ajar, into the Dream that keeps on swallowing and, like a cardboard mask, won't cough me up.

    —*Translated from the Spanish by Stephen Kessler*

(from *Pasión de la tierra*, 1935)

The Body and the Soul

But it is sadder than that, much, much sadder.
Sad as a branch letting its fruit fall for no one.
Sadder, much sadder. Like the mist
the dead fruit breathes out from the ground.
Like that hand that rises from the corpse lying in state
and merely wants to touch the lamps,
the grieving smile, the night speechless and velvet.
Luminous night above the corpse stretched out without its soul.
The soul outside, soul outside the body, swooping
with such delicacy over the shape sad and abandoned.
Soul of soft mist, held floating
above its former lover, the defenseless and pale
body, which grows older as the night goes on,
it remains silent, alone, empty in a gentle way.

Soul of love that watches and hesitates
to free itself, but finally leaves, gentle and cold.

—*Translated from the Spanish by Robert Bly*

(from *Sombra del paraíso,* 1944)

Guitar or Moon

A guitar like the moon.
Is it the moon or only its blood?
It's a tiny heart that has escaped
and goes over the woods trailing its blue, sleepless music.

A voice or its blood,
a passion or its terror,
a fish or a dry moon
that flops about at night, splashing the valleys.

Strange hand or threatening anger.
Is the moon red or yellow?
No, it's not an eye turned bloodshot in its rage
to see the edges of the tiny earth.

Hand that searches through the sky for life itself,
that searches for the heartbeat of a bleeding sky,
that searches deep in the middle of the old planets
who miss the guitar that shines in the night.

Grief, grief of a beast no one can quite describe,
when wild animals feel their hair bristling,
when they feel themselves soaked in the cold light
that hunts for their skins like a monstrous hand.

—*Translated from the Spanish by Lewis Hyde and David Unger*

(from *Mundo a solas,* 1950)

Bent Time

There were years when I was different
or the same. I invented principalities, horrible pedigrees
or a fantastic victory. Sadness all the time.
I loved people I didn't like. And I stopped loving the one I had.
The sea might have been a big wall, maybe a delicate bridge.
Did I know who I was or just learn to forget myself?
Did I honor the fish (lively silver in time)
or was I tyring to domesticate light? Dead words here.
I got up hot with passion and fell quiet with shade, afternoon.
I burned greedily. I did the chant of ashes.
And when I looked into the water, I didn't know who I was.
    Narcissus is sad.
I reported the condition. I cursed the planets
and in my exaggerated style I served what comes
from their useless music, never sure if it was real.
I wanted to drink the shadow of crowds of people
like a man who drinks the water of a trick desert.
Palm trees…Yes, I'm singing…But no one used to listen.
The dunes, the sand used to throb without sleep.
Sometimes I hear a false shadow running
through what's supposed to be a body. Or I go off by myself and
    spit. "Burn yourself up."
But I'm not burning. Sleep, sleep…Yes! "Get it over with."

—Translated from the Spanish by Lewis Hyde

(from *Poemas de la consumación,* 1968)

PERMISSIONS

"Closed," "My Voice," "The Bull," "At the Bottom of the Wall (The Buried Man)," "Flying Fugue for a Horse," "The Body and the Soul," "Guitar or Moon," and "Bent Time"
Reprinted from *A Longing for the Light: Selected Poems,* Vicente Aleixandre, trans. by various translators, edited by Lewis Hyde (New York: Harper & Row, 1979; reprinted by Port Townsend, Washington: Cooper Canyon Press, 1985). Copyright ©1979 by Lewis Hyde. Reprinted by permission of HarperCollins Publications, Inc.

Luis Cernuda (y Bidon) [Spain]
1902-1963

Born in September 21, 1902 in Seville, Spain, Luis
Cernuda was an early member of the Spanish poets
of the so-called "Generation of 1927," which includ-
ed Gabriel García Lorca, Rafael Alberti (see PIP
Anthology, no. 1), Vicente Aleixandre, Jorge Guillén
and many others. He began writing poetry as a law
student at the University of Madrid.

drawing by RAMÓN GAYA

His first work, *Perfil del aire*, showed the influ-
ence of Pedro Salinas, who had helped him to get
the book published, and Cernuda's contemporary
Guillén. But it received only a lukewarm reception.
However in his next, surrealist-influenced writings,
"Un río, un amor" (1929) and "Los placeres pro-
hibidos" (1931) (both collected in *La realidad y el deso* [1936]), he began to find his true voice,
experimenting with incongruous word choices and chance-oriented methods of composition.
Other works such as *Donde habaite el olvido* and *Invocaciones* continued his exploration of
emotional and spiritual autobiographical material, which is at the center of his poems.

Cernuda's open homosexuality and his keen sense of isolation brought on, in part, by the
Spanish Civil War and his insuing exile in Europe, the United States, and Mexico, which began
just prior to the Republican defeat in 1939, focused his poetry on themes of homosexual love
and a strong sense of metaphysical pessimism.

Cernuda's major influences were clearly French, but his own concerns, and his readings of
English and German Romanticism also had a strong effect on his writing. Accordingly, his
poetry often functions as a kind of dialectic, a dialogue between himself as sexual being and
a poet of the mind against the background of mythological, historical, and personal associa-
tions.

He died of a heart attack in Mexico City in 1963.

BOOKS OF POETRY:

Perfil del aire (Málaga: Imprenta Sur, 1927); *Egloga, elegía, oda* (1928); *La invitación a la poesía*
(Madrid: Altolaguirre, 1933); *La realidad y el deseo* (Madrid: Cruz & Raya/Arbol, 1936; revised
and enlarged edition, Mexico City: Tezontle, 1958); *Ocnos* (London: Dolphin, 1942; elarged
edition, Madrid: Insula, 1949; again enlarged, Jalapa, Mexico: Universidad Veracruzana, 1963);
Las nubes (Buenos Aires: Schapire/Rama de Oro, 1943); *Como quien espera el alba* (Buenos
Aires: Losada, 1947); *Variaciones sobre tema mexicano* (Mexico City: Porrúa & Obregón, 1950);
Poemas para un cuerpo (Málaga: Dardo, 1957); *Desolatión de la quimera* (Mexico City: Mortiz,
1962); *Antología poética*, edited by Rafael Santos Torroella (Barcelona: Plaza & Janés, 1970);
Perfil del aire; Con otras obras olvidadas e inéditas, documentos y epistolario, edited by Derek

19

Harris (London: Tamesis, 1971); *Poesía completa,* edited by Derek Harris (London: Tamesis, 1971); *Poesía completa,* edited by Derek Harris and Luis Maristany (Barcelona: Seix Barral, 1974; revised, 1977); *Antología poética, Luis Cernuda,* edited by Philip Silver (Madrid: Alianza, 1975); *Sonetos clásicos servillanos* (Madrid: El Observatorio, 1986); *Poesía Completa,* edited by Derek Harris and Luis Maristany (Madrid: Ediciones Siruela, 1993).

ENGLISH LANGUAGE TRANSLATIONS:

The Poetry of Luis Cernuda, edited and trans. by Anthony Edkins and Derek Harris (New York: New York University Press, 1977); *Selected Poems of Luis Cernuda,* edited and translated by Reginald Gibbons (Riverdale-on-Hudson, New York: The Sheep Meadow Press, 1999).

Remorse in Black Tie

A gray man walks the foggy street.
No one suspects. An empty body,
Empty as plains or sea or wind:
Harsh deserts under unrelenting sky.

It is the past, and now his wings
In shadow meet a pallid force;
thus hesitant remorse, at night,
Brings near its heedless shadow secretly.

Don't take that hand! The prideful ivy
Will rise about the boles of winter.
In calm, the gray man goes unseen.
Do you not hear the dead? But earth is deaf.

—*Translated from the Spanish by Reginald Gibbons*

(from *Un río, un amour*, 1929)

Drama, or a Closed Door

Youth with no escort of clouds,
Walls, that the storms will,
The lamp, outside, like a fan, or in,
With eloquence all declare the obvious:
That which one day weakly gives
Itself over, yes, to death.

Bone crushed by the stone of dreams,
What to do—denied escape—
If not on the bridge that leaps with a flash of light
Between two lies—
The lie of life, or the lie of the flesh?

We know so little!—how to sculpt
Biographies in hostile music;
How to count up affirmations
Or denials, the night's long hair;

How like children to invoke the cold
For fear of going alone into the shadow of time.

—Translated from the Spanish by Reginald Gibbons

(from *Un río, un amour*, 1929)

He Did Not Speak Words

He did not speak words
Merely drew near
                    An inquisitive body
Not knowing that desire is a question
Whose answer does not exist
A leaf whose branch does not exist
A world beneath a nonexistent sky.

Anguish makes its way through the bones
Rises up along the veins
Until it breaks the skin
Fountains of dream made flesh
And questioning the clouds.

A light touch in passing
A quick glance into the shadows
Are enough for the body to split in two,
Greedy to take in
Another dreaming body
Half to half, dream and dream, flesh and flesh,
Alike in form, alike in love, equal in desire.

Even if this were only a wish—
For desire is a question whose answer is unknown.

—Translated from the Spanish by Reginald Gibbons

(from *Los placeres prohibidos*, 1931)

Passion for Passion

Passion for passion. Love for love.

I was in a street of ash, lined with huge buildings of sand. I found pleasure there. I looked at him: in his empty eyes there were two tiny clocks; they ran in opposite directions. He held a flower in the corner of his mouth, bitten and broken. The cape on his shoulders was in shreds.

As he passed, some stars began to die, others were being born. I tried to stop him. My arms hung motionless. I wept. I wept so much I could have filled his empty orbits. Then it was dawn.

I understood why a man is called prudent when headless.

—Translated from the Spanish by Reginald Gibbons

(from *Los placeres prohibidos*, 1931)

Nevada

In the state of Nevada
Railroad lines have names of birds.
There are fields all of snow
And hours of snow.

The transparent nights
Open dream lights over waters,
Over starry roof-tops
Holiday pure.

Tears smile.
Sadness sprouts wings
And wings, as we know,
Bring an inconstant love.

Trees embrace trees.
One song kisses another.
Sadness and joy
Ride the lines.

And always snow lies sleeping
On top of more snow, way over there
In Nevada.

—Translated from the Spanish by Erland Anderson

(from *La realidad y el deseo,* 1936)

Affliction

One day he figured it out:
His arms were only clouds—
With clouds it is impossible
To clasp a body or a fortune
To the quick.

Fortune is round
And slowly counts the summer stars.
Arms as sure as the wind are needed
And a kiss like the sea.

But with his lips
He can do nothing but speak
Words to the ceiling,
Words to the floor,
And his arms are clouds that turn life
Into a sailing wind.

—Translated from the Spanish by Erland Anderson

(from *La realidad y el deseo,* 1936)

Dusk

The way dream
Parts body from soul,
This mist
Separates earth and light:

Everything is blurred and strange;
The silent breeze,
Motionless water
And earth void of color.

Do you know
What that quiet bird
Awaits on its dry twig,
Estranged from itself?

Afar, behind the window
A burning lamp
Makes the hour uncertain.
Life lies

Down, and alone,
Neither living nor dead,
You feel its weak beating
In your body.

You roam these sordid
Outskirts aimlessly
Like the directionless fate
Of man himself.

In your mind, you search
For light or faith,
While outside
Darkness slowly conquers.

—Translated from the Spanish by Reginald Gibbons

(from *Como quien espera el alba*, 1947)

Andrée Chedid [b.Egypt/France]
1920

Born in Cairo, Egypt, Andrée Chedid grew up in a family of mixed Lebanese and Egyptian ancestry. She attended French schools, matriculating at the American University of Cairo. In 1942 she married a physican, Louis Chedid, and moved with him to Paris in 1946.

Chedid had already begun writing poetry, and would continue to publish works from 1949 onward. Her first major book, *Textes pour une figure* (1949) was followed with almost a book a year until the 1990s. Her major collected poems appear in *Textes pour un poème*, 1949-1970, published in 1987.

Chedid also published fiction beginning in 1952 with *Le Sommeil de livre (From Sleep Unbound)*, and through the years has become a major novelist. Her work has been widely translated and established a notable international audience. Among her other works of fiction are *Le Sixieme Jour (The Sixth Day)*, *La Maison sans racines (The Return to Beirut)*, and *L'Enfant multiple (The Multiple Child)*.

Unlike her fiction, grounded as it is in the images and emotions of the Middle East, her poetry, as she describes it, is "free of time and place," having "no geographical boundaries," and belonging "to all lands." Her poetry is often autobiographical, but in its mix of history, fiction, myth and on occasion, magic, is distilled from larger issues.

Chedid is also a well-known dramatist. She continues to live in Paris, where, despite her concerns with her heritage and her knowledge of Arabic, she feels most at home.

BOOKS OF POETRY:

On the Trails of My Fancy (Cairo: Horus, 1943); *Textes pour une figure* (Paris: Pré-aux-Clercs, 1949); *Textes pour un poème* (Paris: Guy Levis-Mano, 1950); *Textes pour le vivant* (Paris: Guy Levis-Mano, 1953); *Textes pour la terre aimée* (Paris: Guy Levis-Mano, 1955); *Terre et Poésie* (Paris: Guy Levis-Mano, 1956); Terre regardée (Paris: Guy Levis-Mano, 1957); *Seul le visage* (Paris: Guy Levis-Mano, 1960); *Double-Pays* (Paris: Guy Levis-Mano, 1965); *Contre-Chant* (Paris: Flammarion, 1968); *Visage premier* (Paris: Flammarion, 1972); *Prendre corps* (Paris: Guy Levis-Mano, 1973); *Voix multiples* (Paris: Commune Measure, 1974); *Fraternité de la parole* (Paris: Flammarion, 1976); *Ceremonial de la violence* (Paris: Flammarion, 1975); *Le Coeur et le temps* (Paris: L'Ecole, 1977); *Le Mort devant* (Paris: Marc Pessin, 1977); *Cadences de l'univers* (Paris: Vodaine, 1978); *Sommeil contradictoire* (Dijon: Brandes, 1978); *Greffes* (Paris: Le Verbe et L'Empreinte, n.d.); *Cavernes et Soleils* (Paris: Flammarion, 1979); *Epreuves du vivant* (Paris: Flammarion, 1983); *Sept Plantes pour un herbier* (Romillé: Folle Avoine, 1983); *Sept Textes pour un chant* (Romillé: Folle Avoine, 1986); *Textes pour un poème,* 1949-1970 (Paris: Flammarion, 1987); *Ancienne Egypt* (Paris: Nouvelles Nouvelles, 1990); *Poèmes pour un texte* (Paris: Flammarion, 1991); *Par delà les mots* (Paris: Flammarion, 1995)

ENGLISH LANGUAGE TRANSLATIONS:

Selected Poems of Andrée Chedid, trans. by Judy Cochran (Lewiston, New York: The Edwin Mellen Press, 1995); *Fugitive Suns: Selected Poetry,* trans. by Lynne Goodhart and Jon Wagner (Los Angeles: Green Integer, 1999)

Mountains

Beneath a sky crackled as a shell
I took the mountain path
To an arid vineyard

There pines bend
And fall into the ravines

Furtive winds breathe in the trace
   of my steps

I run toward the taciturn bridge
Which gathers the abyss

There is no epilogue

Even if the lamb falls from the shoulder of the shepherd
Fleeing in his owls' wing cape

Even if the forked tree
Breaks in two

   —*Translated from the French by Lynne Goodheart and Jon Wagner*

(from *Textes pour un poème*, 1950)

First Image of Revolt

The woman without memories
Has left for the high lands
The ancestors' withered field

In the mornings of wrath
She runs dressed in black
Among the scattered flocks

Nothing is there
But a stark village
Resting heavily on a hill.

—Translated from the French by Judy Cochran

(from *Textes pour le vivant,* 1953)

Land of Omens

Delphi

All we have disappears
What we are remains
Seeding itself even in winter

Light leaning on monsters
The acrid speech of the dead rising
  in the dawn
Here again we want to know

But the sky lowers against these hills
Lost the oracle's cries
The steps of the stranger lost
Soon as well the image
  memory betrays
And we, unable to name our destiny
Lost for words among the shadows
What do we carry to our death?

Perhaps the surf
The cry the ever-cresting fire
This sweetness of another place
Sometimes golden on our lips

Life the lure that leads us on

—Translated from the French by Lynne Goodheart and Jon Wagner

(from *Terre regardée,* 1957)

Land of Dreams

I ran off with the child-king, who believed in the journey.

Over the bleak roofs, I cast our cloak of oblivion.
Then we fled,
Leaving the old oak's torn shadow,
The cries of terror,
The sharp angles of our walls.
On my right shoulder, I carried the child-king.
Our footsteps across the parched land
Were as yielding as the throats of birds.

The child's eyes widened in the sun;
His garden, where silences reside,
Flourishes beneath the tree of life.

Because nothing is simple, I ran off with the child-king.

Now we are together:
  His springtime
  My autumn
  Our magic
  And my step.

—*Translated from the French by Judy Cochran*

(from *Terre regardée*, 1957)

Proofs in Black and Gold

From a distance
Beneath the din of war
The earth moans endlessly

Howls
Savage the seasons
The body stops
Blood hardens
Faces, hands knot

In folds of death

Here
Glistening with green shadows
Enlaced in holiday

Pleasure

Streams down
The shoulders of summer

—Translated from the French by Lynne Goodheart and Jon Wagner

(from *Poèmes pour un texte*, 1991)

Truth

The Truth is nothing but a lie
Tenacious mirage of the living
It mocks our vigilance
And petrifies time

Truth is armed
Its spur the forbidden
Its bronze laws segregate us
Its words have walls and ceilings

Its single target a delusion
Sowings abound
Harvests are legion

Rather let us salute our fugitive suns
Words freed from symbols
Our paths on the move
Our multiple horizons

—Translated from the French by Lynne Goodheart and Jon Wagner

(from *Poèmes pour un texte*, 1991)

Resurrection or Resurrections

I

Before this Resurrection
This wind from other skies
This home in other worlds
This garden of afterward
   whose compost and confines
   escape the eye of the living
   their hearts lined with memory
   their bodies warped by time

Unable to name anything
I feel no call

Imagining these proud spirits
Their space without shores
Trees without season
Mirrors without dust

On the edge of the ultimate country
Where the flowing river
   carries off all silt
Where the bottomless mouth
   swallows up all reflections

Words darken
Vision stops

Ephemeral voyager
I penetrate nothing in this land without flesh
Touch nothing in this place without walls

II

But these daily and prodigious
resurrections
   borne by the dove
   by the surge of blood

Of these resurrections
  drawn from the soul's waves
  and the sowings of the heart

I know the vigor and the taste
I know the ardent return

Secular dawns
  pull us from the swamps
Hands and voices
  dislodge our tombstones
  offer us breath and light
Offer openings from one day to the next
  born from a loving look
  sprung from a word
Light in folds of mist
Rain on our deserts

From little deaths
to brief resurrections

Hours sweep away hours
to the last recital
of the elusive secret

—Translated from the French by Lynne Goodheart and Jon Wagner

(from *Poèmes pour un texte,* 1991)

PERMISSIONS

Oliverio Girondo [Argentina]
1891-1967

drawing by CARLOS ALONSO

Born of a wealthy family in Buenos Aires in 1891, Oliverio Girondo spent his early years in Argentina and Europe, traveling to the Universal Exhibition in Paris in 1900, when he was only nine, and where he later claimed to have seen Oscar Wilde stalking the streets with sunflower in hand. After spending some time at the Lycée Louis le Grand in Paris and Epsom school in England, he made an agreement with his family to attend law school in Buenos Aires if they would send him each year to Europe for the holidays. For the next several years, Girondo explored the continent, even traveling to find the source of the Nile.

Meanwhile, back at home he had begun writing avant-garde plays, which caused a stir in the theater world of Argentina. In 1922 he published, in France, his first volume and verse, *20 Poems to Be Read in a Streetcar*, which shows the influence of the Appolinaire and the Parisian scene. Only in 1925, with the second printing of this book, did Girondo receive attention in Argentina. By this time, the Ultraists, lead by Jorge Luis Borges, had become a major force on the scene, and Girondo continued his own humorous exploration of the aesthetic in his second volume, *Decals*. In the same period he became involved with the avant-garde journal *Martín Fierro*, which brought together younger poets such as Girondo and Borges with more established figures such as Ricardo Güiraldes and Macedonio Fernández.

After a five year period of traveling again, Girondo returned to Buenos Aires, publishing two of his major works, *Espanatapájaros (Scarecrow)* (1932) and *Interlunio (Intermoonlude)* (1937). A new book, *Campo nuestro (Our Countryside)*, appeared in 1946, the same year he married the poet Nora Lange. In this new work he moved away from the Ultraist ideas, playing with elaborate metaphoric language. As Borges moved toward his more fantasist works, and a new generation of poets arose, Girondo was increasingly described as a humorous or even frivolous poet, but his 1956 work, *Moremarrow* stood as a darker summation of his career, a work that bears comparison with the great Chilean writer Vicente Huidobro's *Altazor*. However, many readers feel that Girondo went further in his linguistic explorations. During that same period Girondo revived the journal *Contemporánea*.

In 1964 Girondo was hit by a car, and for the several years suffered terrible pain before dying of those injuries in 1967. His last works were gathered by the surrealist poet Enrique Molina.

BOOKS OF POETRY:

Viente poemas para ser leídos en el travía (Argenteuil, France: C. H. Barthélemy, 1922);

35

Calcomanías (Madrid: Editorial Calpe, 1925); *Espantapájaros* (*Al alcance de todos*) (Buenos Aires: Editorial Proa, 1932); *Interlunio* (Buenos Aires: Editorial Sur, 1937); *Persuasión de los días* (Buenos Aires: Editorial Losada, 1942); *Campo nuestro* (Buenos Aires: Editorial Sudamericana, 1946); *En la masmédula* (Buenos Aires: Losada, 1954, 1956, 1963); *Obras completas* (Buenos Aires: Losada, 1968); *Obra completa* (Madrid: Galaxia Gutenberg, 1999).

ENGLISH LANGUAGE TRANSLATIONS:

Scarecrow and Other Anomalies, trans. by Gilbert Alter-Gilbert (Riverside, California: Xenos Books, 2002).

```
              I      know   nothing
             You     know   nothing
             Thou  knowest  nothing
             He     knows   nothing
             Men    know    nothing
             Women  know    nothing
             You all  know  nothing
           None of us knows anything at all.
```

The disorientation of my generation has its explanation
in the direction of our education, whose idealization
of action, was — without question! — a mystification,
    in distinction to our passion for meditation,
        contemplation and masturbation.

```
        (Guttural, as  guttural  as can be.)
         I believe I believe in that which
          I  believe  I  do  not  believe.
          And I believe I don't believe
           in what  I believe I believe.
```

```
          "Song       of  the      froggies"

         A      A      Is  Is      A     A
          nd     nd     it  it      nd    nd
          a      be     th  thi     a     be
          bove   low    ere ther    bove  low
          the    the    ?   ?       the   the
          stair  lad    It          It    stair lad
          ways   ders   is          is    ways  ders
          climb  cur    n't         n't   climb cur
          ing    ving   he          hi    ing   ving
          over   under  re          ther  over  under
          head!  neath! !           !     head! neath!
```

—*Translated from the Spanish by Gilbert Alter-Gilbert*

(from *Espantapájaros* , 1932)

8

I don't have a personality: I am a cocktail, a conglomerate, a riot of personalities. In me, personality is a species of inimical furunculosis in a chronic state of eruption; not a half hour can pass without my sprouting a new personality.

Whenever I think I am alone, the assembled host surrounds me, and my house looks like the consulting room of a fashionable astrologer. There are personalities everywhere: in the reception room, in the halls, in the kitchen, even in the W.C....

It's impossible to strike a truce, or find a moment's rest! It's impossible to know which one is the real me!

Although I see myself forced to live in the most abject promiscuity with them, I am not convinced that they have anything to do with me.

What connection can they possibly have — I ask myself — all these univited, unconfessed personalities, so bloodthirsty they could make a butcher blush with embarrassment? How can I allow myself to identify, for example, with this shrivelled-up pederast who didn't even have the courage to act it out, or with this cretinoid whose smile could freeze a speeding locomotive?

The fact that they inhabit my body is enough, however, to make me sick with indignation. Since I cannot ignore their existence, I want to make them hide in the inmost convolutions of my brain. For they have to do with a certain petulance...a certain selfishness...a certain absence of tact....

Even the most insignificant personalities arrogate to themselves certain cosmopolitan airs. All of them, without exception, consider themselves entitled to display an Olympian disdain for the others, and naturally there are quarrels of all sorts, interminable disputes and disagreements. You'd think they might have some grounds for compromise, adopt some means of living together, but no, sir, each one claims the right to impose its will, without taking into account the opinions and tastes of the others. If one of them cracks a joke that makes me break out laughing, during the act another comes out to propose a little stroll through the cemetery. Nor is it good that the former wants me to go to bed with every woman in the city, while the latter attempts to show me the advantages of abstinence; and while one takes advantage of the night and does not let me sleep until dawn, the other wakes me at daybreak and insists that I get up with the chickens.

My life thus becomes a breeding of possibilities that are never realized, an explosion of opposing forces that conflict and collide in the process of mutual destruction. The attempt to make the least decision causes me such a mass of difficulties, before undertaking the most insignificant act I must put such personalities in accord, so that, frankly, I prefer to give up everything and wait from them to get tired of arguing over what they have to do with my person, in order to have, at least, the satisfaction of consigning one and all to the shitcan.

—*Translated from the Spanish by Gilbert Alter-Gilbert*

(from *Espantapájaros* , 1932)

12

They admire, they desire, they gravitate
they caress, they undress, they osculate
they pant, they sniff, they penetrate
they weld, they meld, they conjugate
they sleep, they wake, they illuminate
they covet, they touch, they fascinate
they chew, they taste, they salivate
they tangle, they twine, they segretage
they languish, they lapse, they reintegrate
they wriggle, they squirm, they infundibulate
they fumble, they fondle, they perficate
they swoon, they twitch, they resuscitate
they sulk, they pout, they contemplate
they ignite, they inflame, they incinerate
they erupt, they explode, they detonate
they nab, they grab, they dislocate
they clinch, they clutch, they concatenate
they solder, they dissolve, they calcinate
they paw, they claw, they assassinate
they choke, they shudder, they federate
they redden, they madden, they federate
they repose, they loll, the oscitate
they splice, they smolder, they colligate
they abate, they alate and they transubstantiate.

—*Translated from the Spanish by Gilbert Alter-Gilbert*

(from *Espantapájaros* , 1932)

18

Weep living tears! Weep gushers! Weep your guts out! Weep dreams! Weep before portals and at ports of entry! Weep in fellowship! Weep in yellow!

Open the locks and canals of tears! Let us soak our shirts, our souls! Inundate the sidewalks and the boulevards, and bear us along safely on the flood!

Assist in anthropology courses, weeping! Celebrate relatives' birthdays, weeping! Walk across Africa, weeping!

Weep like a caiman, like a crocodile....especially if it's true that caimans and crocodiles have no real tears in them.

Weep anything, but weep well! Weep with your nose, with your knees! Weep through your navel, through your mouth!

Weep of love, of hate, of happiness! Weep in your frock, from flatus, from frailty! Weep impromptu, weep from memory! Weep throughout the insomniac night and throughout the livelong day!

—Translated from the Spanish by Gilbert Alter-Gilbert

(from *Espantapájaros,* 1932)

21

May noises bore into your teeth like a dentist's drill, and may memory fill you with rust, broken words and the stench of decay.

May a spider's foot sprout from each of your pores, may you find nourishment only in packs of worn cards and may sleep reduce you, like a steam roller, to the thickness of your photograph.

When you step into the street, may even the lampposts dog your heels, may an irresitible fanaticism oblige you to prostrate yourself before every garbage pail and may all the inhabitants of the city mistake you for a urinal.

When you want to say "My love," may you say "fried fish"; may your own hands try to strangle you at every turn, and every time you go to flick away a cigarette, may it be you who is hurled into the spittoon.

May your wife deceive you even with the mailboxes; when she snuggles next to you, may she metamorphose into a blood-sucking leech and, after giving birth to a crow, may she bring forth a monkey wrench.

May your family amuse itself deforming your bone structure, so that mirrors, looking at you, commit suicide out of sheer repugnance; may your only entertainment consist of installing yourself in the waiting rooms of dentists, disguised as a crocodile, and may you fall so passionately in love with a toolbox that you can't desist, even for an instant, from licking its clasp.

—*Translated from the Spanish by Gilbert Alter-Gilbert*

(from *Espantapájaros*, 1932)

Invitation to Vomit

Cover your face
and cry.
Vomit.
Yes!
Vomit,
thick slivers of glass,
bitter straight pins,
worm-eaten words,
stifled shrieks of fright;
puke on this pus-flood of innocence overflowing its banks,
this slime of sickening iniquity sloshing from its trench,
and this fetid, denatured submissiveness brewed
from a flatulent broth of terror and starvation.

Cover your face
and cry...
but don't hold back.
Vomit.
Yes!
Vomit,
retch in the face of this macabre paranoiac stupidity,
heave all over this delirious stentorian cretinism,

and this senile orgy of prostatic egotism:
foul coagulations of dried-up disgust,
pulped hulks of impotence already drowned
in a rancid gravy of boredom,
rotten chunks of soured hope...
hours split open by neighings of anguish.

—*Translated from the Spanish by Gilbert Alter-Gilbert*

(from *Persuasión de los días,* 1942)

The Pure No

The no
the novarian no
the cease aryan no
the nooo
the post-mucosmos of animalevolent zero no's that no no no
and nooo
and monoplurally no to the morbid amorpus nooo
nodious no
no deus
no sense no sex no way
the stiff no bones about it nooo in the unisolo amodule
no pores no nodule
nor me nor man nor *mal*
the no no macro dirt
the no greater than all no things
the pure no
the no bull

—*Translated from the Spanish by Eliot Weinberger*

(from *En la masmédula,* 1954)

Sodium Pentothal So What

So what's not gloomy about the lay
the harmony so what the strain

they had possessed
the head-on gasping grasping sub-sucking smacks
the skinquakes
the spiritual scuba
the honeycomb-come so what
coming so what to the finish line
relapsing lapping weighed down so what what larva the tedious
    tongue-twisting in poisonous cubes
so many others others
thirst so what
X's
the dizzy nexus
the taste of so what nakedness
the stubborn stillborn helliday with the kids
the exnubile pros
giving yourself to give to what
the endless accompaniments
the undressed wounds
the pounding impounding
the warping warp in the daily Sing Sing of the blood
the ideonecrococci with their ancestors of dirt
to be so what
or not to be so what
tough luck
the slow summing shrinking
the veneral Avernos
the fish in the nau-sea for what
whosoever so what's whoever
so many sowhats

so what

  so what

  so what

  and yet

—*Translated from the Spanish by Eliot Weinberger*

(from *En la masmédula*, 1954)

PERMISSIONS

[I know nothing], [8], [12], [18], and [21] from *Scarecrow* and "Invitation to Vomit"
Reprinted from *Scarecrow and Other Anomalies,* trans. by Gilbert Alter-Gilbert (Riverside, California: Xenos Books, 2002). Reprinted by permission of Xenos Books and the translator.

from "The Pure No" and "Sodium Pentothol So What"
Reprinted from *The Borzoi Anthology of Latin American Literature, Vol. II,* edited by Emir Rodriguez Monegral (New York: Alfred A. Knopf, 1977), pp. 623-624. Oliverio Girondo trans. by Eliot Weinberger. Reprinted by permission of Eliot Weinberger.

Miguel Hernández [Spain]
1910-1942

drawing by ANTONIO BUERO VALLEJO

Born into a peasant family in Orihuela in south-eastern Spain, Miguel Hernández spent much of his youth as a goatherd and performing other farming tasks. But as young boy Hernández determined to become a poet, despite his father's attempts to dissuade him and to follow more practical activities. At the age of nine he began his schooling at the school annex for poor children, Escuela del Ave María. By 1923, at the age of 13, the young student, excited by Spanish literature, was honored by an invitation to study at the nearby Colegio de Santo Domingo de Orihuela, attended previously by the novelist Gabriel Miró. The Jesuits who ran school encouraged him to seek the priesthood, but at the age of 15, his father took him out of school to help in herding and selling milk.

In the years immediately after leaving school Hernández befriended members and friends of the Fenoll family, who ran the local bakery. Carlos Fenoll and Sijé were drawn to Hernández because of his poetry and quickness of mind, and together these three regularly met, reading their plays and poetry to one another. Sijé, in particular, became Hernández's mentor, encouraging him to study Spanish poetry in depth and arranging for him to perform his poetry at the Casino.

In 1931 the young poet traveled to Madrid to make his way among the more cosmopolitan writers; but he found the large metropolis unfriendly, and returned to his country home. One of Hernández's poems was published just before his return in *Gaceta Literaria*, but the attention it brought was not enough to keep him longer in Madrid. He borrowed a railway ticket from a friend; without the legal travel documents, however, he was arrested en route by the Guardia Civil and imprisoned.

Back in Oriheula he worked as a bookkeeper for a fabric company and, later, as a clerk in a notary's office. He continued his study, during this period, of the Spanish poetic tradition, in particular Góngora and his imitators, Gerardo Diego and Rafael Alberti (*PIP Anthology*, volume 1). Although in the more sophisticated circles the Góngora tradition was waning, the young poet, through a loan from the publisher Raimundo de los Reyes, published his first book *Perito en lunas* (1933). Accordingly, the book did not receive the attention he expected, and the hermetic style of the poems was beyond most uninitiated readers. Although the book was not successful it did push Hernández toward a full career as a poet.

In 1934, through a local benefit performance on his behalf, the young poet was able to afford to return to Madrid, living modestly in the city. He was now known by several poets and gained deeper acquaintance to García Lorca, Alberti, Jorge Guillén (*PIP Anthology*, volume 1),

Luis Cernada, and others. Two other poets he now met, Pablo Neruda (*PIP Anthology*, volume 2) and Vicente Aleixandre, became important figures in his life, particularly Aleixandre, who, as Hernández was drawn further into the group of poets with Republican and socialist leanings, replaced Sijé—with whom Hernández had a gradual and long falling out—as his mentor.

In 1936 Hernández was again arrested during a trip to San Fernando del Jarama for not having the proper identification papers. Only a phone call to Neruda in Madrid secured his release. This second arrest would radically affect the rest of his life. For in July of that year an uprising led by Generalissimo Francisco Franco in the North African province of Melilla caused services in Spain to come to a standstill. Lorca, visiting his Andalusia, was captured by the military and killed along with others in Granada. By September Madrid was in the throes of the Spanish Civil War, and Hernández enrolled in the Fifth Regiment of the Republican forces, fighting the Nationalists and Franco near the town of Cubas. Taken ill, he returned to Madrid where he joined the First Calvary Company of the Peasants' Battalion and read poetry daily on radio. As cultural affairs officer, he also traveled extensively, reading to the soldiers new war poems as he wrote them. In November, he performed with a Cuban officer, Pablo de la Torriente Brau, at an event attended by Alberti and others. Three weeks later Brau was killed. Others were also fast disappearing: Neruda accepted a post in Paris and the great poet Macado moved to Valencia; Ortega left Spain and Unamuno died in December, under house arrest.

In March of 1937 Hernández married his beloved girlfriend from Oriheula, Josefina. In April he was forced to return to his regiment, and four days later he heard the news that Josefina's mother had died. Working on the proofs of his next book, *Viento del pueblo*, Hernández tried to release his mind from the series of tragic events surrounding him.

Viento del pueblo was published to mostly positive reviews, and in the months just before Hernández had become deeper and deeper involved in the Republican activities, including participation in a International Writers' Congress (which included notables André Malraux, Octavio Paz, Cesar Vallejo, Stephen Spender, and Jean Cassou) and a trip to the Fifth Festival of Soviet Theater in Moscow. The new book showed the influence of his Madrid friends and war activities. The formal concerns of his first volume were abandoned as he wrote in free verse and employed more popular forms such as the romance and political commentary. As his first son was born, Hernández was already at work on his next volume, *El hombre acecha*, which would be published in 1939. Ten months later the son died, and the father fell sick in Benicasim while Hernández was writing one of his most memorable poems, "A mi higi" ("To My Son"). His second son was born in January 1939, at a time when the exodus of of people fleeing the country was quickly mounting. Machado's death in France in January was another event to strongly effect Hernández; although he collected the galleys for *El hombre acecha*, the book was never bound nor published. He now felt fear for his own and family's survival. In April he crossed the border to Portugal, but was spotted by a police patrol and arrested. Soon after, he was sent to Torrijos Prison in Madrid, where he was held from May to September. Keeping in touch with Aleixandre, Hernández received as much support as possible, but things grew worse and his wife was denied her mother's pension. Hernández was released, possibly by beaucratic mistake, in September; but as he traveled to Josefina in Cox, his enemies in the Franco-supporting Oriheula were already plotting. While visting the Sijé family in Orihuela, Hernández was arrested and imprisoned. In December 1939 he was transferred to the Conde de Poreno Prison in Madrid, where in the company of fellow prisoner Buero Vallejo, the poet continued to discuss his art and write.

For the next two years, in and out of solitary confinement, Hernández was kept in prison, where he wrote long letters to his wife and son and composed more poetry. He 1942, suffering from tuberculosis, he died.

BOOKS OF POETRY:

Perito en lunas (Murcia: Sudeste, 1933); *En rayo que no cesa* (Madrid: Héroe, 1936); *Viento del pueblo* (Valencia: Socorro Rojo, 1937); *El hombre acecha* (Valencia: Subsecretaría de Propaganda, 1939); *Sino sangriento y otros poems* (Havana: Verónica/Altolaguirre, 1939); *Seis poems inéditos y nueve más*, edited by Vicente Ramos and Manuel Molina (Alicante: Ifach, 1951); *Anthología poética de Miguel Hernández*, edited by Francisco Martínez Marín (Orihuela: Aura, 1951); *Obra escogida*, edited by Arturo del Hoyo (Madrid: Aguilar, 1952); *Cancionero y romancero de ausencias*, edited by Elvio Romero (Madrid: Arión, 1957); *Los mejores versons de Miguel Hernández*, edited by Manuel Molina (Buenos Aires: Nuestra América, 1958); *Los hijos de la piedra* (Buenos Aires: Quetzal, 1959); *Obras completas*, edited by Elvio Romero and Andrés Ramón Vázquez (Buenos Aires: Losada, 1960); *Antología*, edited by María de Gracia Ifach, 1961); *Canto de independencia* (Havana: Tertulia, 1962); *Poemas de adolescencia: Perito en lunas; Otros poemas* (Buenos Aires: Losada, 1963); *El hombre acecha; Cancionero y romancero de ausencias; Últimos poems* (Buenos Aires: Losada, 1963); *Imagen de tu hella; El rayo que no ceas; Viento del pueblo; El Siblo vulnerado; Otros poemas* (Buenos Aires: Losada, 1963); *Poemas*, edited by José Luis Cano and Josefina Manresa (Barcelona: Plaza & Janés, 1964); *Poesía* (Havana: Consejo Nacional de Cultura, 1964); *Poesías*, edited by Jacinto Luis Guereña (Paris: Seghers, 1964; Madrid: Taurus, 1967; enlarged, Madrid: Narcea, 1973); *Unos poemas olvidados de Migue Hernández*, selected by A. Fernández Molina (Caracas: Universal, 1967); *Cinco sonetos inéditos*, compiled by Dario Puccini (Caracas: Revisa Nacional de Cultura, 1968); *Poemas de amor*, edited by Leopoldo de Luis (Madrid: Alfaguara, 1969); *Obra poética completa*, edited by Luis and Jorge Urrutia (Bilbao: Zero, 1976); *Poesía y prosa de guerra y otros textos olvidados*, edited by Cano Ballesta and Robert Marrast (Pomplona: Peralta, 1977); *Poemas sociales de guerra y de muerte*, edited by Leopoldo Luis (Madrid: Alianza, 1977); *Poesías completas*, edited by Sánchez Vidal (Madrid: Aguilar, 1979)

ENGLISH LANGUAGE TRANSLATIONS:

Songbook of Absences: Selected Poems of Miguel Hernández, trans. by Thomas C. Jones, Jr. (Washington, D.C.: Charioteer, 1972); *Miguel Hernández and Blas de Otero: Selected Poems*, edited by Timothy Baland and Hardie St. Martin [trans. by Timothy Baland, Hardie St. Martin, Robert Bly, and James Wright] (Boston: Beacon, 1972); *Unceasing Lightning*, trans. by

Michael Smith (Dublin: Dedalus, 1986); *Selected Poems of Miguel Hernández,* edited by Timothy Baland [trans. by Timothy Baland, Robert Bly, Hardie St. Martin, and James Wright] (Fredonia, New York: White Pine Press, 1989); *The Unending Lighting: Selected Poems of Miguel Hernández,* trans. by Edwin Honig (Riverdale-on-Hudson, New York: Sheep Meadow Press, 1990); *I have Lots of Heart: Selected Poems,* trans. by Don Share (Newcastle upon Tyne, England: Bloodaxe Books, 1997); *The Selected Poems of Miguel Hernández,* edited by Ted Genoways, trans. by various translators (Chicago: University of Chicago Press, 2001).

4

You tossed me a lemon, it was so sour,
with a warm hand, it was so white,
it never bruised the fruit's skin
but the bitterness was what I could taste.

With one golden blow, my blood
was aroused from slow sweetness
to a fever hot pitch when that hard teat
bit back at the tip of my tongue.

But glancing up to see you smile
at what the lemony act had made
of my maliciously sly intent

I felt my blood sink in my shirt,
and that soft and jaundiced breast
squirt a peculiarly sharp pain.

—*Translated from Spanish by Douglas Messerli*

(from *El rayo que no cesa,* 1936)

11

It kills me, you're so pure and chaste:
though I confess, my love, I'm guilty,
I snatched that kiss; yes, it was I
who sipped the flower of your face.

I sipped the flower of your face,
and since that great day and deed
your face, so weighty and so scrupulous,
droops, falling like a yellow leaf.

The ghost of that delinquent kiss
now haunts your cheekbone, growing ever
darker, heavy and immense.

How jealously you stay awake!
How zealously you watch my lips
against (God forbid) another break!

—Translated from the Spanish by Edwin Honig

(from *El rayo que no cesa*, 1936)

Child of the Night

Laughing and playing in the sharp light of day,
the child I twice wanted to be sank into the night.
He no longer wanted the light. What for? He wouldn't leave
those silences, that dark gloom, again.

I wanted to be...What for? I wanted to come joyfully
into the heart of the sphere of all that exists.
I wanted to bring with me laughter, most beautiful thing.
I died smiling, serenely sad.

Child twice a child: a third time on the way.
Circle once again that opaque world of the womb.
Stay back, love. Stay back, child, since I wouldn't
come out where light meets its heavy sorrow.

I go back to the shaping air that fed my unawareness.
I go circling back, aware of my cover of sleep.
In a sensuous, dark transparency,
to roam an interior space, October to October.

Womb: core flesh of all that exists.
Vault eternally dark, whether blue or red.
Night of nights, in whose depths one feels
the voice of roots, the breath of heights.

Under your skin I press on, the distance is blood.
My body swings in a dense constellation.
The universe sets off its floating echoes
in the place where the history of man is written.

To gaze and see surrounding solitude, mountain,
sea, through the window of one full heart
that yesterday grieved not to be an horizon
opening on a world less changeable, transient.

To hoard, for no reason, the stone and the child:
just to live one day without wings in the dark.
Pillar of frightening salt, cut off
without fresh air or fire. No. Life, go back.

But something has desperately hurtled me on.
In the past, the dawning of time, I fall.
I am hurled out of the night. And in the wounding light
naked I weep again, as I always have wept.

—Translated from the Spanish by Edwin Honig

(from *Cancionero y romancero de ausencias,* 1958)

Lullaby of the Onion

An onion is frost
shut tight and poor.
Frost of your days
and my nights.
Hunger and onion,
black ice and frost
large and round.

My child lay there
in his cradle of hunger
and nursed on
the blood of an onion.
But your blood
was a frost of sugar
on onion and hunger.

Dissolved into moon,
a dark-haired woman
lets trickle by trickle
spill over the cradle.

Little one, laugh,
you can eat up the moon
whenever you want.

Lark of my house,
laugh again and again,
Laughter's the light
of the world in your eyes.
Keep laughing so that
in my soul when it hears you
space will be conquered.

Your laughter frees me,
lends me wings,
cancels loneliness,
tears down my prison,
lets my mouth fly, lets
heart touch your lips
flashing lightning.

Laughter's your most
victorious weapon,
conquering flowers
and larks,
rivalling suns,
future of all my bones
and my love.

Flesh quivering,
suddenly blinking,
child never blushed
with such color.
So many linnets
flutter, fly up
from your body.

I awoke from being a child:
you never waken.
My mouth is sad.
You always laugh!

In your cradle always
defending laughter
feather by feather.

Keep soaring so high
and so far
you become flesh
of the just-born sky.
If I could only
go back to the start
of your flight!

Eight months and your laughter,
five lemon blossoms.
Five of the tiniest
ferocities.
Those five teeth of yours
five adolescent
jasmines.

Tomorrow they'll arrive at
the frontier of kissing
when you will sense
in your teeth a weapon,
sense fire flow down
from those teeth
avidly seeking a center.

Little one, fly on
the double moon of the breast:
it, an onion sad and poor;
you, fed and content.
Do not falter.
Never mind what happens
or what's to come.

—*Translated from the Spanish by Edwin Honig*

(from *Cancionero y romancero de ausencias*, 1958)

Gyula Illyes [Hungary]
1902-1983

Gyula Illyes was born in Rácegres, Hungary on November 2, 1902. His father (an agricultural machinist) was a Catholic, while his mother, a servant, was Calvinist. Living on an estate which was run in almost feudal manner, Illyes experienced both traditional forms and the need for rebellion. In his youth, he joined the revolutionary army, but when proletariat dictatorship collasped in 1919, he was forced into exile, during which time he attended the Sorbonne of the University of Paris, while at the same time working as a miner, a bookbinder and a teacher. During this period he encountered French Surrealism, which influenced his earliest poems.

Illyes returned to Hungary in 1926, when he worked as a clerk. But his passion was still writing, and when the great Hungarian author Mihály Babits offered him a regular space in the avant-garde monthly *Nyugat,* Illyes began contributing poetry, addressing Hungarian problems in a surrealist manner. Through these writings the young author became known as a spokesman for the peasantry, living at the time under near serf-like conditions.

His first book of poetry was *Nehézföld,* published in 1928, in which he decried the conditions of the peasants. Further exploring the theme in his prose work *Puszták népe* was published in 1936 *(The People of Pusztak,* 1967) in which he recalled the events of his youth, exposing the terrible conditions of the peasants. As a result of this argument and his continued fight for better conditions for the peasantry, Illyes was elected to the Hungarian Parliment in 1945.

After the Communist takeover in 1947, Illyes's anti-Marxist views brought attack from party leaders, and he was silenced. But gradually, as writers began speak out again in the mid-1950s, Illyes took a central position in declaring revolution, and during the 1956 revolution published the famous poem "One Sentence of Tyranny" (written in 1951) that continues to stand as a masterwork of Hungarian modernism. When the revolution was crushed, he was again silenced, writing major works of poetry in private. In 1948, 1953, and 1970, Illyes won the Kossuth Prize for Literature, and in 1965 he received the Maison Internationale de la Poesie (in Brussels) International Grand Prix.

He died in 1983.

BOOKS OF POETRY :

Nehéz föld (Budapest: Nyugat, 1928); *Három öreg* (Budapest: S. Szerző 1932); *Hősköröl beszélek* (Cluj-Koloszvár: Korunk 1933); *Ifjuság* (Debrecen: Nagy Károly és Társai, 1934); *Szálló egek alatt* (Budapest: Nyugat, 1935); *A kacsalaba fargo var* (Budapest: 1936); *Nem menekulhetsz* (Budapest: 1936); *Rend a romokban* (Budapest: Nyugat, 1937); *Külön világban* (Budapest, Cserépfelvi, 1939); *Összegyüjött versek* (Budapest: 1940); *Egy év* (Budapest: Sarló, 1945); *Megy az eke* (Budapest, 1945); *Szembenézve* (Budapest: Revai, 1947); *Tizenkét nap Bulgáriában* (Budapest: 1947); *Összes versei* (Budapest, 1947); *Két kéz* (Budapest: Athenaeum, 1950); *Illyes Gyula válogatott versek* (Budapest: 1952); *A casudafurulyás juhász* (Budapest: Ifjúsági 1954); *Oda Bartokhoz* (Budapest: 1955); *Egy mondat a zsamoksagrol* (Budapest: 1956); *Kézfogások* (Budapest: Magvetö Konyvkiadó, 1956); *Uj versek* (Budapest: Szépirodalmi Konyvkiadó, 1961); *Nem volt elég* (Budapest: Szépirodalmi Konyvkiadó, 1962); *Nyitott aftó* (Budpaest: Europa Konyvdiadó, 1963); *Dőlt vitorla* (Budapest: Szépirodalmi Konyvkiadó, 1965); *A kolto felel* (Budapest: Athenaeum Nymoda, 1966); *Poharaim* (Budapest: Szépirodalmi Konyvkiado, 1967); *Fekete-Feher* (Budapest: Szépirodalmi Knoyvkiadó, 1968); *Abbahagyott versek* (Budapest: Szépirodalmi Knoyvkiadó, 1971); *Haza amagasban: Összegyüjött versek, 1920-1945* (Budapest: Szépirodalmi Knoyvkiadó, 1972); *Minden lehet* (Budapest: Szépirodalmi Knoyvkiadó, 1973); *Teremteni: Osszegyujott versek* (Budapest: Szépirodalmi Knoyvkiadó, 1973); *Illyes Gyula Összegyüljött versei* (Budapest: Szépirodalmi Knoyvkiadó, 1977); *Nyitott ajtok: Osszegyujtott versforditasok* (Budapest: Szépirodalmi Knoyvkiadó, 1978)

ENGLISH LANGUAGE TRANSLATIONS:

A Tribute to Guyla Illyés, edited by Thomas Kabdebo and Paul Tabori (Washington, D.C.: Occidental Press, 1968); *Selected Poems*, edited by Thomas Kabdebo and Paul Tabori (London: Chatto & Windus, 1971); selections in *Modern Hungarian Poetry*, edited by Miklós Vajda (New York: Columbia University Press, 1977); selections in *In Quest of The Miracle Stag: The Poetry of Hungary*, edited by Adam Makkai (Chicago: Atlantis-Centaur,/Budapest: Corvina Publishers, 1996); selections in *The Colonnade of Teeth: Modern Hungarian Poetry*, edited by George Gömöri and George Szirtes (London: Bloodaxe Books, 1996); *What You Have Almost Forgotten: Selected Poems by Gyula Illyés*, edited by William Jay Smith (Budapest: Kortárs Kiadó/Willimantic, Connecticut: Curbstone Press, 1999); *Charon's Ferry*, translated by Bruce Berlind (Evanston: Illinois: Northwestern University Press, 2000)

The Apricot-Tree

1

The apricot-tree
shoulder-high or less—
Look! an apricot
at branch-tip ripeness.

Stretching, straining,
holding out a prize,
the tree is a maiden
offering closed eyes.

You stand and wonder:
will she bend or sway
her slender waist or
step back, run away.

With quick breath shudders
from heat or passion,
fans herself, signals
in the high fashion.

Shakes the shimmering
pomp out of her dress,
then blushing she waits
for your compliments.

This garden a ballroom.
she gazes about,
anxiously, constantly,
wants to be sought out.

2

I spend each evening
all evening with her.

Come again tomorrow
she says in whisper.

She rustles softly
when I salute her.
It seems my poetry
can still transmute her.

Sweet apricot-tree,
in a dream I saw
the cool arbor, and you
on the crackling straw.

First you glanced around
anxiously, then left
the dark hedge, the well,
in your moon-white shift.

Your steeping increased
the silence gently,
brought me your body
soft and sweet-scented.

Since that dream I glance
towards you, flushing.
Please look at me too,
askance and blushing.

(1937)

—*Translated from the Hungarian by Christine Brooke-Rose*

Horror

I saw: Budapest burning:
around a people's head
before its fall, a glowing
wreath of fire; war; war dead.

I saw—as if someone else—
amid wild briarbush

of exploding shell, a corpse,
a nightmare carcass, crushed.

There was moonlight that morning
six o'clock, New Year's day;
the housewreck I was standing
on, at dawn, turned grey.

Like Moses' bushes, burning,
each shell, with rapid shriek
burst, screaming something—
God or Fate tried to speak.

In the icy snow of the street
I saw a human head,
a bas-relief trampled flat
by some inhuman tread.

I saw a baby, still blind,
close to its dead mother:
not milk to suck but blood,
blood not wool for cover

The baby raised its bloody face
and cried out to the dead.
His mother was—, this very place;
himself— the years ahead.

(1945)

—Translated from the Hungarian by Anthony Edkins

Grass Snake and Fish

Among pebbles, at the pond's edge,
      in limpid shallows whose water
flows as transparent as the atmosphere,
      suddenly visible

in that world made for other lungs,
      living purity, where

the stone wavers in the drift
    of the reflection, a branch in air;

into that shut Eden, slides the snake,
    guided by the oldest law:
a fish palpitates hanging from its fangs
    howling what no one can translate.

(1956)

—Translated from the Hungarian by Charles Tomlinson

Logbook of a Lost Caravan

Only the compass, keeping hope alive,
    stuttered on, uttering its paralyzed
directions; with something somewhere beyond
    to which to respond.

    And for another long day
we struggled ahead through desert sand.

Then to the edge of stone cliffs
    covered with hieroglyphs.

Line after line, incoherent, they read—
    wrinkles on some mad forehad.

    An ancient age
struggled there in desperate tones—

With nothing more to say—

    And only the wind moans.

Sand in our eyes. Between sweating fingers, and
    ground between teeth, sand.

We slaughtered the camel who knew the way…
had our final meal today.

(1965)

—*Translated from the Hungarian by William Jay Smith*

While the Record Plays

They heated hatchet blades over gas fires in roadside
    workshops and hammered them into cleavers.

They brought wooden blocks on trucks and carried
    them across these new provinces grimly, quickly,
    and steadily: almost according to ritual.

Because at any time—at noon or midnight—they would
    arrive at one of these impure settlements,

where women did not cook nor make beds as theirs
    did, where men did not greet one another as they
    did, where children and the whole damned company
    did not pronounce words as they did, and where
    the girls kept apart from them.

They would select from these insolent and intolerable
    people twelve men, preferably young ones, to take
    to the marketplace,

and there—because of *blah-blah-blah* and moreover
    quack-quack-quack and likewise *quack-blah-quack*—
    would beat and behead them,

of historical necessity—because of *twaddle-twiddle* and
    twiddle-diddle, and expertly, for their occupations
    would be different one from the other.

agronomist and butcher, bookbinder and engineer,
    waiter and doctor, several seminarists, cadets from
    military academies, a considerable number of students,

those familiar with Carnot, Beethoven and even
   Einstein, displaying their finest talents,

because, after all, nevertheless, *blah-blah-blah* and
   twiddle-dee-dee,

while through loudspeakers records played—music and
   an occasional gruff order, and they, the zealous
   ones, wiped their foreheads and turned aside
   every now and then to urinate since excitement
   affects the kidneys;

then having washing the blocks and hauled down the
   large tricolor which on such occasions always
   waved above their heads,

they too would march on into the broad future,

past the heads, carefully placed in a circle,

then out of the settlement where now also

and forever and ever,

reason, comfort, and hope would be no—

wrr-wrr-wrr—that is to say—*we-ep, wa-rp,* the sound (by
   now the only one without music or words) that the
   needle makes as the record grinds on.

(1965)

—*Translated from the Hungarian by William Jay Smith*

Charon's Ferry

Charon's ferry does not depart with us when
    our eyes have closed and iced over.
Mournful crossers, it's for long and with eyes wide open
    we move on the fateful water.

Our jealous destiny drives us, years before,
    into the boat; and we rock with it.
It glides—though not to our liking—along a shore
    equally exquisite;

equally beautiful as on lagoons or *canali*,
    those of honeymooners.
Surely it's all the same: sky, journey, scenery
    —only in reverse!

Everything's equally exquisite, if fact—mystically—
    as it fleets away, more exquisite even!
Something like what happens to a melody
    when it leaves the violin.

Laughing, we sit among friends and trees
    —cheerful gibes go around—
and all of a sudden the ferry begins to rock with us
    (just us!), outward bound.

He's wise who smiles at the pleasure cruise.
    When he weeps, his tears should then
be in thanks for so many piazzas, such Casa d'Oros,
    though he won't see them again.

—Translated from the Hungarian by Bruce Berlind

Successful Effort

The ship went down, with a big bump reached the bottom of the sea, and keeled over. It now turns out that it was a country, a nation. "After a hurricane." I was a passenger, but somehow or other—due to sheer chance or because, in spite of the storm, I'd gone up on deck to look around—a current (I held on to the railing in vain) carried me up to the surface. The sun was shining. Yachts were racing on the calmed water. My friends, flying along in a boat, cried out in a foreign language, but so clearly, in words as cleanly luminous as the sparkles of sun on the rippling water. Of the shipwreck—or even of the storm—they knew nothing. I laughed, I drank—the ambrosial Banyuls. And because—again by sheer chance—I knew how to handle the sails, I could become, then and there, a happy member of the *équipage*. Together we took possession of the wreath of victory.

It took me five years and a thousand tricks to get back to the ship on the bottom of the sea, where whoever hadn't perished had gone mad.

—*Translated from the Hungarian by Bruce Berlind*

PERMISSIONS

Kusano Shinpei [Japan]
1903-1988

Kusano was born in Nagano in 1903, and at the age of 18 moved to Canton, China. It was there he graduated from Lingnan University, where he learned his English. The stay in China brought a closer relationship to Chinese literature than perhaps for any other Japanese poet, and Kusano drew upon Chinese words throughout his writing career. In 1935, he and friends founded the monthly magazine *Rekitei* (Historical Process), which grew eventually into a poetry group of over one thousand members.

He returned to Japan in 1939, but because of World War II, published very little new work until the late 1940s. Among his many works from 1948 to the time of his death were *Botan En* (1948, Peony Garden); *Kowareta Orugan* (1968, The Broken Organ); *Zenten* (1975, The Entire Firmament); *Ken'kon* (1979, Heaven and Earth); *Unki* (1980, Cloud Passage); *Gengen* (1981, Pitch Pitch); *Genjō* (1982, Mysterious Lute); *Mirai* (1983, The Future); *Genten* (1984, Northern Frimament); *Genkei* (1985, Dreamscape); and *Jimon Tamon* (1986, Asking Myself/Asking Another). His collected writings appeared as *Kusano Shinpei Zenshū* in 1978-84.

Kusano became a very popular poet throughout Japan, and Japanese school children all knew his poems about frogs. He was a frequent talk show vistor, and the Royal family often sought him out for occasional poems.

BOOKS OF POETRY:

Daihyaku Kaikyō (1928); *Botan En* (1948); *Kowareta Orugan* (1968); *Zenten* (1974); *Ken'kon* (1979); *Unki* (Tokyo: Chikuma Shobō, 1980); *Gengen* (Tokyo: Chikuma Shobō, 1981); *Genjō* (Toyko: Chikuma Shobō, 1982); *Mirai* (Tokyo: Chikuma Shobō, 1983); *Genten* (Tokyo: Chikuma Shobō, 1984); *Kusano Shinpei Zenshū* (Tokyo: Chikuma Shobō, 1978-1984); *Genkei* (Tokyo: Chikuma Shobō, 1985); *Jimon Tamon* (Tokyo: Chikuma Shobō, 1986).

ENGLISH LANGUAGE TRANSLATIONS:

Frogs & Others, trans. by Cid Corman (New York: Grossman, 1969); *Asking Myself, Answering Myself*, trans. by Cid Corman (New York: New Directions, 1984); *Mt. Fuji—Selected Poems 1943-1985*, trans. by Leith Morton (Rochester, Michigan: Katydid Books, 1991)

Mulligan Stew Feast

12 Nov. 1977 from morning and all day—cloudless sky.
Just right for a mulligan stew feast.
After 10 a.m. S turned up, then, H, W and also (woman) S.
Today's lot have all been connected to the farm.
Mulligan's stew's at night, before that, some heavy jobs.
1. Removing the red bricks on the west side of the garden and
     digging from there to the concrete fence transplant
     zephyranthus candida to the edges.
2. Beside the compost pit dig another hole and put the flower-
     pots into it.
3. Beside them arrange red bricks in a row and make a common
     grave for the animals.
4. Pull up the eggplants. In their place sow silver beet and
     garden-pea seeds.
5. Dig up the taro.
6. Shift the earth dug out of the holes to the rose garden.
7. On the east side make an oven with bricks and rocks.
8. Take the dead leaves from the garden to the compost pot.
9. Clean out the pond do the weeding etc.
Everyone grabbed spades, hoes and pruning shears and began to
work.
The old man from Koenuma brought bundles of straw on his
     bicycle to protect the peonies against frost.
We were covered in sweat, bathed in the sunlight from a cloudless
     sky.
Time for a breather.
Spreading two mats on the paddock we sit cross-legged.
Slurping hot noodles.
Then back to work.
We go and get a long plank from a nearby builder and cut it
     with a saw.
Give it a good scrub and dry it in the sun.
Upstairs I write on a grave marker.

Kōzō Fū Kō Gen Pen Tonko

KUSANO FAMILY TOMB

Black Fuji and the rest all the fishes Amen

Into a gap in the square of red brink. I hammer it deeply.
The work in the paddock and garden is mostly finished.
I set fire to some dead wood in our improvised oven.
W brought thick pieces of charcoal from the cellar.
A rare treat in times like our own.
Chucked them over four or five pieces of burning wood.
On top of that plonked a massive iron pot 62 cms in diameter and
    filled with water.
Tables and giant *saké* bottles and beer and glasses and chopsticks.
We all split up to carry them.
The water in the iron pot had boiled and was chattering and
    bubbling away.
The seasoning was my responsibility.
First Shinshū miso paste and chopped pork.
Then in the pot went most respectfully the taro radish and mustard
    rape dug up this morning.
Next in particular order came the food in baskets and on trays.
Burdock. Carrots. Tōfu. Chinese Cabbage. Cabbage. Mushrooms.
    Devil's tongue.
Kidney Beats. Shallots. Komatsuna Cabbage.
I tasted some from a small dish. On top I poured beer and *saké*.
And a few tiny drops of soy sauce.
First I put some half-boiled vegetables and rice into a bowl and placed
    it on the Kusano family tomb as an offering.
Just then simply and directly we
Toasted each other with beer and saké.
A big steaming bowl was passed from hand to hand.
After that came eating and drinking. Drinking and eating.
The sun was already orange and was about to sink on the southern
    flank of Fuji.
The giant size candles bought at Tsubekawa in Izu were brought out.
Also a big square candle pink and white and light blue all mixed
    together made for me by a young woman I didn't know.
Anyhow we all unabashedly
scream out "tastes great" "lovely."
So it ought.
After the work an open-air feast.
But we couldn't eat everything in the massive 62 cm pot.
Ended up getting the neighbors in to share it.
Sun set and candlelight flared.
Bodies and faces glowed.

Moon came up.
Charcoal crackled.
Carefully dowsed the fire.
Afterwards decided to continue the party upstairs.

—*Translated from the Japanese by Leigh Morton*

(from *Ken'kon*, 1979)

For Riley Kelly Lee and Yamada Ichimuraski's Shakuhachi and Single-String Koto Performance of "Budding"

With a single bamboo and.
A single string and.
Into space.
The sound of Japan rises.

The transparent sapphire.
Sound of Japan rises.
Flowing out.

—*Translated from the Japanese by Leigh Morton*

(from *Mirai*, 1983)

Birthday Party

between sandbanks marsh reflecting twilight clouds.
purple mist rising.
the golden moondish risen.

bulrush and sedge marshedge.
on stalk leaf tip velvet pile of fireflies.
firefly light quick quick off/on.
on waterbeetle back waterspider. on catfish whiskers
    glimmering duckweed.

then.
equisetum flute fluted all around.
and all at once the marsh face full of frog faces.

making many circles solemnly quietly.
fireflies all together turn out their lights.
all around the darkness springs up.
equisetum flute flutes again shrill all around.
Jubliee for the End of the Endless Serene 10,000 Years' Choir
    bulrush booming swaying all over.

that's Gobila stood up maybe.
or Glimma or Qayloqay maybe.
in flickerings the choir ends.
unusually tall zebra grass pressing against.
after chanting deep bara-a-ra-bara-a.

all our births'.
all our joys'.
one night of the year tonight.
all our hearts beating.
all our eyes flashing.
celebrating all our futures.
all of us....

drink and sing. buddies—jabojabojabo—jabo light's
    whirlpool.

killifish glitteringly splash
innumerable fireflies streaming mingle.

li- li-   lililu lililu liffuffuffuff'
li- li-   lililu lililu liffuffuffuff'

lilinf fkenk'
fkenk' kekekke
kekukku kekukku kensalili-olu
kekukku kekukku kensalili-olu
biida-lala biida-lala
binbin begank'
biida-lala biida-lala
binbin begank'
begank' begank' gaggaga-lili-ki
begank' begank' gaggaga-lili-ki
galili-ki kikukku gaggaga-lili-ki
galili-ki kikukku kukkuku gugugu
kikukku kukukku kukkuku gugugu

gugugu gugunk'
gugugugu gugunk'
gululut gululut iiiiiiiiiiiiiiii
gululut gululut iiiiiiiiiiiiiiii
gamb'yan gamb'yan
our dream.
color of dawn.
our song
gamb'yan gamb'yan

gyawalot'gyawalot'gyawa-lolololoi(t)
gyawalot'gyawalot'gyawa-lolololoi(t)
gyawalot'gyawalot'gyawa-lolololoi(t)
gyawalot'gyawalot'gyawa-lolololoi(t)
gyawalot'gyawalot'gyawa-lolololoi(t)

gyawalot'gyawalot'gyawa-lolololoi(t)
gyawalot'gyawalot'gyawa-lolololoi(t)
gyawalot'gyawalot'gyawa-lolololoi(t)
gyawalot'gyawalot'gyawa-lolololoi(t)
gyawalot'gyawalot'gyawa-lolololoi(t)
gyawalot'gyawalot'gyawa-lolololoi(t)
gyawalot'gyawalot'gyawa-lolololoi(t)

epilogue

as author I have no desire to stop the choir at
this party celebrating birth. on the banks of
O-Aza Kamigawa in the village of Kamiogawa in
the district of Iwaki in the prefecture of Fuku-
shima. a party of points tinier than seasame seed
as yet. this ectasy's swaying echoing flowing place.
but actually snow sifting outside, me in my poor
kotatsu, sitting crosslegged in heavy dark. med-
itation ending with what was born. (in my body some
of the singing staying. now fair faint ripples.) O
already the strung lights of the fireflies have all
gone out. a tangle of torn goldfish-weed only catching
vainly at the big full moon.

—*Translated from the Japanese by Cid Corman*

Mystery of White & Green

of a pale snowy luster &.
pungency & sweetness.

under earth white swelling.
above earth green stretching.

(why do white & green divide)
(why do white & green unite)

this fresh mystery.

as far as.
as far as.
radish field.

—Translated from the Japanese by Cid Corman

Sea Bream

fierce tough burly bony sea bream.
spiky fins. visored head.
scaly flesh of the fierce streamlined fish.

big red sea bream left on the chopping board untouched
    for a time
let the knife wait.

winter light collecting on the streamlined fish.
red. vermilion. gold. purple.
diffused reflections.
yellow speckles.
bandit of the Pacific.
eyes forever wide.
glistening.

—Translated from the Japanese by Cid Corman

Hachijo Rhapsody

dadadan dadadan dadadan dadadan dan dan
dan dan dan dan dah dah dah

night wind licking the Kurashio crawls over the field &.
three bonfires blaze.
cra-ra-rackling.
swinging flames.
    dan dan dan dan
boys leopardskins round their waists.
drumsticks carving the wind &.
    dan dan dadadan
(dancing dance barebreasted crescent moon clinging there.)
August's great festival of life.
dance. drink. devour. drink. devour. dance.
a giant tossing rotten dry mackerel into his gaping gullet.
(and *tagobe* too. taro. and so much bamboo-shoot potato.)
from a *Jomon* cup demon-killing liquor.
big women drinking up brims of rice-brandy. (hot mist
burning belly) young female deer. imps snivelling.
let yourself go old women! topaz women.
dance dance.

    wheel of the sun ah-doro ah-doro ah-doro
    wheel of the moon ginga ginga ginga.
    praised be heaven and earth!
    o Gods. sing.

lice in wild stringy hair clinging to the shaking in crawling
    into pores &.
crescent jade necklace swinging at breasts yun yun pulling
    torn off.

    dan dan dan dan dan dan dan kakaka dan
    kakaka dan kakakakakah dan kakakat dan dan kat
    dan ka dan dan dan dan dan dan dan dan dan kakakat

oh. praise fire.
praise wind.
praise water.
praise earth.

praise sea-turtle and wild grass.
praise the life in all that lives.
praise cunnus and phallus.

dan dan dadadan

Brahms' satellite rising.
from the dead end of heaven's line.
along the shores of the Milky Way.
through the center of the Swan's belly and lost in the depths
of heaven.
oh. the long past and the long future commingle and make
what is new strong. da da da.
yesterday and today languishing here and there make what is
new weak. da da da.
bonfires blazing crackle.

(pasania-wood. camphorwood burn anything.)
dan dan dan dan
Hachijo night unadvancing.
Brahms' satellite!
Kojiki friend!

dan dan dan dan dadadan dadadan
dah dah dah dah dadadan dah dada

—*Translated from the Japanese by Cid Corman*

PERMISSIONS

"Mulligan Stew Feast" and "For Kelly Lee and Yamada Ichimurasaki's Shakuhachi and Single-String Koto Performance of 'Budding'"
Reprinted from *Mt. Fuji—Selected Poems* 1943-1985, trans. by Leith Morton (Rochester, Michigan: Katydid Books, 1991). Copyright ©1991 by Leith Morton. Reprinted by permission of Katydid Books.

"Birthday Party," "Mystery of White & Green," "Sea Bream," and "Hachijo Rhapsody"
Reprinted from *asking myself, answering myself*, trans. by Cid Corman with Susumu Kamaike (New York: New Directions, 1984). Copyright ©1969, 1978, 1980, 1984 by Cid Corman. Reprinted by permission of New Directions Publishing Corporation.

Else Lasker-Schüler [Germany]
1859-1945

drawing by PAUL LASKER-SCHÜLER

"The Black Swan of Israel" and "The greatest lyric poet of modern Germany" are two of the epithets used to describe the poet Else Lasker-Schüler. "The subject of her poems was mainly Jewish, her imagination essentially oriental, but her language was German," wrote Gottfried Benn (see *PIP Anthology,* volume 2).

Lasker-Schüler was born into a bourgeois family of German-Jewish origin in the provincial town of Wuppertal-Elberfeld on February 11, 1869. Her father, Aaron Schüler, was a private banker with connections to the building trade. In the poet's autobiographical writings, he is described as a playful, affectionate and not quite grown-up eccentric. Her mother, Jeanette Kissing, a great admirer of Goethe and Heine, encouraged her daughter's early attempts at writing poetry. The harmony of this idyllic existence was disrupted by the death of her favorite brother, Paul, in 1882, and the death of her mother in 1890, from which she never fully recovered. For Lasker-Schüler, death was a reality which she had to turn into fantasy to be able to bear.

In 1894, Else Schüler married Dr. Berthold Lasker and moved to Berlin. But five years later, the marriage ended, marking a rupture with conventional values and the beginning of a bohemian existence which she was to lead for the rest of her life. A year later, Lasker-Schüler gave birth to her son, Paul, allegedly fathered by one Alcibiades de Rouan. The affair remains clouded in mystery.

Styx, her first book of poetry, was published in 1902. Certain general themes which appear in this early volume were to recur throughout her poetic career: loneliness and disillusionment in love, an ardent desire to reach beyond mere personal relationships to a greater spiritual communion, a sensual and inventive use of language, and the creation of an extravagant personal mythology. Nor was this mythicizing penchant restricted to her art alone.

She married George Levin, the famous art critic and composer, in 1902, renaming him Herwath Walden. He was one of the leading promoters and theoreticians of the German Expressionist Movement, as well as the founder of their major journal, *Der Strum* (also named by Lasker-Schüler) in which she published her poems.

After the break-up of her second marriage in 1911, the poet's life became even more unstable. Most of her days and nights were spent at the same Berlin café which she described as "our nocturnal home…our oasis, our gypsy caravan, our tent in which we can rest after the painful battles of the day." It was here that she wrote the poems of her Expressionist volume, *My Wonder* (1911) and became intimately acquainted with many of the great artists of the period: George Trakl; Gottfried Benn, with whom she had a tempestuous love affair; Franz Marc; Karl

Kraus; Oscar Kokoschka; Georg Grosz; and Franz Werfel. Several of the poems in this work are about or dedicated to these artists.

By 1913, though already a celebrity in the German-speaking world, Lasker-Schüler was living in loneliness and destitution. The poet's son, Paul, a gifted artist who meant more to her than any other living being, died in 1927, at the age to twenty-eight. After this loss, the poet turned even more inward, immersing herself more deeply in Jewish tradition, especially in mysticism and the Kabbalah.

In 1932, Lasker-Schüler was awarded the prestigious Kleist Prize for literature. However, when Hitler came to power several months later, the sixty-four-year old poet was beaten by a group of Nazis with an iron rod. Without so much as returning to her room, she ran to the station and took the first train out of Germany to Zürich.

After several years as a vagabond, Lasker-Schüler emigrated to Palestine in 1939, and founded a literary group called "Der Kraal," where she would read her poems by candlelight, often accompanied by little bells and a harmonica. In Jerusalem, as in Berlin, Lasker-Schüler was regarded as an eccentric personality, still clad in her fairy-tale dresses, jewelry and masks, convinced that she was Jussuf of Thebes or Tino of Baghdad, living in an unheated room without even a bed, decorated with puppets and toys.

It was during her last years in Jerusalem that she wrote possibly her most famous book of poetry, *My Blue Piano* (1943). Many of the poet's earlier concerns and images recur in this last volume, but with a density and, frequently, a calm largely absent in her earlier writings.

On January 22, 1945, she died after suffering a severe heart attack. She was accorded the rare honor of being buried on the Mount of Olives.

—JEANETTE LITMAN-DEMEESTÈRE AND PEGGY FRANKSTON

BOOKS OF POETRY:

Styx. Gedichte (Berlin: Axel Juncker Verlag, 1902); *Der siebente Tag. Gedichte* (Berlin: Verlag des Vereins für Kunst, 1905); *Meine Wunder. Gedichte* (Karlsruhe/Leipzig: Dreililien-Verlag, 1911); *Hebräische Balladen* (Berlin: A. R. Meyer Verlag, 1913); *Die gesammelten Gedichte* (Leipzig: Verlag der Weiszen Bücher, 1917); *De gesammelten Gedichte* (Leipzig and Munich: Kurt Wolff Verlag, 1920); *Hebräische Balladen. Der Gedichte erster Teil* (Berlin: Verlag Paul Cassirer, 1920); *Die Kuppel. Der Gedichte zweiter Teil* (Berlin: Verlag Paul Cassirer, 1920); *Mein blaues Klavier. Neue Gedichte* (Jerusalem: Jerusalem Press, 1943)

ENGLISH LANGUAGE TRANSLATIONS:

Hebrew Ballads and Other Poems, trans. by Jeanette Demeestère-Litman and Audri Durchslag-Litt (New York: The Jewish Publication Society of America, 1980); *Stars in My Forehead: Selected Poems* trans. by Janine Canan (Duluth, Minnesota: Holy Cow! Press, 1999); *Selected Poems*, trans. by Jeanette Demeestère-Litman and Audri Durchslag-Litt [enlarged and revised from *Hebrew Ballads and Other Poems*] (Los Angeles: Green Integer, 2002).

My Drama

With all sweet-scented scarletflowers
He lured me.
I could not bear this narrow room for one more night;
Before his door I stole crumbs of love
And, longing for him, consumed my life.
A pale angel weeps softly within me,
Buried—I believe deep in my soul,
       He stands in dread of me.
In wild weather I saw my face!
I don't know where, perhaps in dark lightning,
My eye frozen in my countenance, like a winternight;
I never saw a grief more grim.
…With all sweet-scented scarletflowers
       He lured me.
Again the pain stirs in my soul
And guides me through all remembrance.
Be still, my wild angel mine,
       God weep not,
     Say nothing of the sorrow,
My anguish must not burst forth.
No more faith have I in Woman and Man,
The cord, that tied me to all life,
I gave back to the world
       Willingly!
Out of every sphinxstone my sorrow will burn,
Blaze around all blossoms, like a black spell.
I long for my blind, cast-out solitude,
To find solace, to embrace it, like my child.
I learned to hate my womb, my heart's blood, and him,
       Never to know Eve's blood—so much
       As in you, Man!

—*Translated from the German by Audri Durchslag-Litt and Jeanette Demeestère-Litman*

(from *Styx,* 1902)

Chronica

Mother and father are in heaven—
   Amen.
Out of silent morning dreams
Three souls suffuse
God's land with tender sorrow—
For three sisters are we,
Who dreamed of old, in sphinxlike shape,
In Pharaoh's time;—
I was formed in the deepest womb of the world
By the most tenacious artist-hand.
And do you know who my brothers are?
They were the three Magi who journeyed east
Following the white star to God's child.
But eight fates festered in our blood.
Four plague us in the evening red,
And four make dark our morning glow,
Bringing upon us hunger's dread,
Heartgrief and death.
So it is written:
Above our final grave they still endure,
Weaving the curse upon all worlds
To rejoice in their evil.
Even the winds will shy away from their dust.
Satan, have mercy.

      *—Translated from the German by Audri Durchslag-Litt and Jeanette
      Demeestère-Litman*

(from *Styx*, 1902)

Homesickness

I do not know the speech
of this cool land,
Nor can I keep its pace.

I cannot even decipher
The drifting clouds.

The night is a step-queen.

I can't stop thinking of Pharoah's woods
And kiss the images of my stars.

My lips already radiant
Speak of distances.

I am a painted picturebook
Upon your lap.

But your face weaves
A veil of tears.

The corals were torn
From my iridescent birds,

By the garden hedges
Their tender nests turn to stone.

Who will anoint my dead palaces—
They wore the crowns of my fathers,
Whose prayers drowned in the holy river.

> —*Translated from the German by Audri Durchslag-Litt and*
> *Jeanette Demeestètre-Litman*

(from *Meine Wunder,* 1911)

The Voices of Eden

Wilder, Eve, more erring, admit
Your longing was the serpent,
It's voice wound over your lip,
And bit into the seam of your cheek.

Wilder, Eve, more voracious, admit
The day you wrested from God,
You looked upon the light too soon,
And sank into the blind caldron of shame.

Immense,
It wound out of your womb,
At first, like a hesitant fulfillment,
Then seizing itself impetuously,
Created itself,
A godlike soul…

And it grows
Over and beyond the world,
Losing its beginnings,
Beyond the boundaries of time,
And back around your thousandfold heart,
Towering above the end…

Sing, Eve, your fearful song, lonely,
Lonelier, dropping leaden, like your heart beats,
Loosen the dark cord of tears,
Strung round the nape of the world.

Like the moonlight, vary your countenance,
You are lovely…
Sing, sing, listen—the rustling sound—
That night plays, oblivious to all.

Everywhere the deaf din—
Your fear rolls over the steps of earth
Down God's spine.

Hardly a hairsbreadth between him and you.
Couch yourself deep in the night's eye,
Let you day wear the dark night.

Heaven suffocates, inclining to the stars—
Eve, the shepherdess, the blue doves
Coo in Eden

Eve, turn around before the last badge!
As you go, cast no shadow,
Wither away, temptress.

Eve, you over-ardent listener,
Oh, you cluster of whitened foam
Flee, even your eyelash's fine cutting edge!

> —*Translated from the German by Audri Durchslag-Litt and Jeanett Demeestère-Litman*

(from *Meine Wunder*, 1911)

George Grosz

Sometimes colored tears play
in his ashen eyes.

But he always encounters hearses;
They scare his dragonflies away.

He is superstitious—
—Born under a great star—

His script, a downpour;
His drawings, opaque letters.

His subjects swell with size.
As though they had long lain in the stream.

Mysterious vagabonds with tadpole mouths
And putrefied souls.

Five dreaming pallbearers
Are his silver fingers.

There is no light within his errant fairytales
And yet he is a child,

The Leatherstocking hero
On intimate terms with the Indian tribes.

Generally he despises all people,
They bring him ill-luck.

But George Grosz loves his misfortune
Like a clinging adversary.

And his sorrow is dionysian;
Black champagne, his lamentation.

He is a sea with a shrouded moon.
His God only seems to be dead.

> —*Translated from the German by Audri Durchslag-Litt and
> Jeanette Demeestère-Litman*

(from *Meine Wunder,* 1911)

Parting

But you never came with the evening—
I sat waiting in a shawl of stars.

…Whenever there was a knocking at my door,
It was my own heart.

It now hangs on every doorpost,
Even on yours;

Between the ferns the fireroses expire
In the withering garland.

I dyed the heaven blackberry
With my heartblood.

But you never came with the evening—
…I stood waiting in golden shoes.

> —*Translated from the German by Audri Durchslag-Litt and
> Jeanette Demeestère-Litman*

(from *Meine Wunder,* 1911)

Reconciliation

Into my lap a great star will fall...
We would waken the night,

And pray in tongues
Carved like harps.

We would be reconciled in the night—
So much of God overflows.

Our hearts are children
Who, weary-sweet, would rest.

Out lips would kiss each other,
What do you fear?

Does my heart not verge on yours—
Your blood still stains my cheeks red.

We would be reconciled in the night,
If we embrace, we shall not die.

Into my lap a great star will fall.

> —Translated from the German by Audri Durchslag-Litt and
> Jeanette Demeestère-Litman

(from *Hebräische Balladen,* 1913)

Abel

Cain's eyes do not please God,
Abel's countenance is a golden garden,
Abel's eyes are nightingales.

Abel always sings so clearly
To the chords of his soul,
But through Cain's body run the city's trenches.

And he will slay his brother—
Abel, Abel, how deeply has your blood stained heaven.

Where is Cain, now that I would smite him:
Did you slay the sweet bird
In your brother's countenance?!!

> —*Translated from the German by Audri Durchslag-Litt and Jeanette Demeestère-Litman*

(from *Hebräische Balladen*, 1913)

My Blue Piano

At home I have a blue piano
But have no note to play.

It stands in the shadow of the cellar door,
There since the world's decay.

Four star-hands play harmony
—The Moon-maiden sang in her boat—
Now rats fandango on the keys.

Broken is the keyboard...
I weep for the blue dead.

Ah, dear angel, open to me
—I have eaten bitter bread—
Heaven's gate, while I'm still alive,
Even against the law's decree.

> —*Translated from the German by Audri Durchslag-Litt and Jeanette Demeestère-Litman*

(from *Mein blaues Klavier*, 1943)

To Me

My poems, declaimed, jar out of tune the keyboard of my heart. If only they were still my children, clinking needfully on my rhymes. (Please don't tattle!) Left behind, I still sit on the last bench in the school-room, as before…But with mellowed heart: 1000 and 2 years old—fairy tales springing up over my head.

I roam all around! My head flies away like a bird, dear mother. Nobody shall spirit away my freedom—should I die somewhere at the road's rim, dear mother, you'll come and carry me up to the blue heaven. I know you were touched by my lonely floating and the playful tick-tock of mine and my dearest child's heart.

> —*Translated from the German by Audri Durchslag-Litt and Jeanette Demeestère- Litman*

(from *Mein blaues Klavier,* 1943)

PERMISSIONS

Mina Loy [England/ USA]
1882-1966

Born in London in 1882, Mina Gertrude Lowy stud-
ied art in Munich and in London (where she was
taught by Augustus John) before moving to Paris in
1903. In Paris she married Stephen Haweis, and
changed her surname to Loy. Her first child, Oda,
died on her first birthday.

The same year Loy met Gertrude and Leo Stein,
and through Stein's salons, met Apollinaire,
Picasso, Rosseau and many others. As her art began
to be noticed in Paris, she moved with her husband
in 1906 to Florence, during which she suffered from
depression and ill-health.

However, Loy continued to produce art and began
to flourish under the influence of Mabel Dodge, who have moved to Florence in 1910. In 1913
Loy exhibited paintings in London, and the same year, Stein and Toklas visited Loy in
Florence. The same year, Loy's husband sailed to the Fiji Islands, Tahiti, Australia, San
Francisco, and New York, and Loy filed for divorce, allying herself with the Italian Futurists.
Over the next few years, despite the declaration of war, and the breaking up of the
American/English colony in Florence, Loy remained, having affairs with the Italian Futurist
writers F. T. Marinetti and Giovanni Papini. As her writing began to be circulated in the avant-
garde circles of New York, Loy grew restless in Italy and began to make plans to go to the
United States. Disillusioned with Futurism, she performed anti-Futurist works such as her
experimental verse play *The Paperers*, which exaggerated masculinities. In October of that
year, 1916, she sailed, with her two children, for New York.

Loy immediately made a sensation in Greenwich Village and in the avant-garde magazine
Others. After she appeared as the wife in Alfred Kreymborg's play *Lima Beans* (William Carlos
Williams was the husband), the New York press "discovered" her. In numerous articles and
editorials throughout 1917, Loy was discussed as the paradigm of the modern woman. That
same year, she met the Dadaist poet-publisher-pugilist-hoaxer Arthur Cravan; they were mar-
ried in Mexico City in January 1918. As Loy sailed for Buenos Aires in preparation for their
return to Europe, Cravan disappeared, never to be seen again.

Back in Europe, Loy began designing lamps and other commercial furniture, and returned
to the social whirl of Paris literary life. As Robert McAlmon reported about her wit at parties
—and her friendship with Djuna Barnes—"If only Djuna Barnes or Mina Loy turned up, the
evening might be saved." Throughout the next decades Loy worked on her poetic masterwork,
Anglo-Mongrels and the Rose.

In 1936 she returned to the United States, forming a lasting friendship with Joseph Cornell
and retaining occasional contacts with friends from Europe, including Djuna Barnes, Marcel

Duchamp, Alfred Kreymborg, Henry Miller, Man Ray and Mary Reynolds. In 1944 she became a naturalized citizen. She died in September 1966 in Aspen, Colorado.

BOOKS OF POETRY:

Lunar Baedeker (Paris: Contact Publishing Company, 1923); selections from "Anglo-Mongrels and the Rose" in *Contact Collection of Contemporary Writers* (Paris: Three Mountains Press, 1925); *Lunar Baedeker and Time-Tables* (Highlands, North Carolina: Jonathan Williams Publisher [Jargon 23], 1958); *The Last Lunar Baedeker,* edited by Roger L. Conover (Highlands, North Carolina: The Jargon Society, 1982); *The Lost Lunar Baedeker,* selected and edited by Roger L. Conover (New York: Farrar, Straus and Giroux, 1996).

Lunar Baedeker

A silver Lucifer
serves
cocaine in cornucopia

To some somnambulists
of adolescent thighs
draped
in satirical draperies

Peris is livery
prepare
Lethe
or posthumous parvenues

Delicious Avenues
lit
with the chandelier souls
of infusoria
from Pharoah's tombstones

lead
to mercurial doomsdays
Odious oasis
in furrowed phosphorous— — —

the eye-white sky-light
white-light district
of lunar lusts

— — — Stellectric signs
"Wing shows on Starway"
"Zodiac carrousel"

Cyclones
of ecstatic dust
and ashes whirl
crusades
from hallucinatory citadels
of shattered glass
into evacuate craters

A flock of dreams
browse on Necropolis

From the shores
of oval oceans
in the oxidized Orient

Onyx-eyed Odalisques
and ornithologists
observe
the flight
of Eros obsolete

And "Immortality"
mildews. . .
in the museums of the moon

"Nocturnal cyclops"
"Crystal concubine"
— — — — — —
Pocked with personification
the fossil virgin of the skies
waxes and wanes— — — —

(from *Lunar Baedeker,* 1923)

Ignoramus

Shut it up

Sing silence
To destiny
Give half-a-crown
To a magician
Half a glance
To window-eclipse
And count the glumes
Of your day's bargaining
Lying

In the lining
Of your pocket
        While compromising
Between the perpendicular and horizontal
Some other tramp
Leans against
The night-nursery of trams

Puffs of black night
Quiver the neck
of the Clown of Fortune
        Dribble out of his trouser ends
In dust-to-dust
Till cock-kingdom-come-crow
You can hear the heart beating
Accoupling
of the masculine and feminine
Universal principles
Mating
And the martyrdom of morning
Caged with the love of houseflies
The avidity of youth
And incommensuration.

Day-spring
Bursting on repetition
        "My friend the Sun
        You have probably met before"
Or breakfasting on rain
You hurry
To interpolate
The over-growth
Of vegetation
With a walking-stick

Or smear a friend
With a greasy residuum
From boiling your soul down
        You can walk to Empyrean to-gether
Under the same
Oil-silk umbrella

"I must have you
Count stars for me
Out of their numeral excess
Please keep the brightest
For the last

(from *Lunar Baedeker*, 1923)

Virgins Plus Curtains Minus Dots

Latin Borghese

Houses hold virgins
The door's on the chain

"Plumb streets with hearts"
"Bore curtains with eyes"

Virgins   without dots*
Stare   beyond probability

See the men pass
Their hats are not ours
We   take a walk
They are going somewhere
And they   may look everywhere
Men's eyes   look into things
Our eyes   look out

A great deal of ourselves
We offer to the mirror
Something less to the confessional
The rest   to Time
There is so much   Time
Everything is full of it
          Such a long time

*Marriage Portions

Virgins may whisper
'Transparent nightdresses made all of lace'
Virgins may squeak
'My dear   I should faint'
Flutter....flutter....flutter....
....'And then   the man---'
Wasting our giggles
For we have no dots

We have been taught
Love is a god
White   with soft wings
            Nobody shouts
            Virgins for sale
Yet where are our coins
For buying a purchaser
Love is a god
      Marriage expensive
A secret well kept
Makes the noise of the world
Nature's arms spread wide
Making room for us
        Room for all of us
Somebody who was never
                    a virgin
Has bolted the door
Put curtains at our windows
See the men pass
They   are going somewhere

Fleshes like weeds
Sprout in the light
So much flesh in the world
                Wanders at will

Some   behind curtains
Throbs to the night
Bait   to the stars
Spread it with gold
And you carry it home
Against your shirt front
To   a shaded light
With the door locked

Against virgins who
Might   scratch

(from *The Last Lunar Baedeker*, 1982)

Gertrude Stein

Curie
of the laboratory
of vocabulary
  she crushed
the tonnage
of consciousness
congealed to phrases
  to extract
a radium of the word

(from *The Last Lunar Baedeker*, 1982)

I Almost Saw God in the Metro

In that state of animated coma
the condition of clochard
this gray-head slumped on a platform bench
like the Emperor of Void
on a throne to which no one pretends
is wrapped in aloofness august
as deity—
an inordinate flower
opening undefiled
among ordure.

(from *The Last Lunar Baedeker*, 1982)

Ceiling at Dawn

Afloat in oval of unclosing eye

white-washed shadow-drifts
of indoor dawn
film idle clouds—

a Cinema-Nirvana
shifts
pallid ideograms
and epitaphs of dreams

upon a white slab slanted.

Visual echoes
in blanched rows

—the dissolved, derouted
traffic of slumber—

an acrid air-flower
adrowse in the etiolate pasture
of our arousing

as droning day
dilates
in early light
the spectral acre

under the sunless artiface
of this four-cornered sky,

lingering flies
convolve their slim-winged circles

(from *The Last Lunar Baedeker*, 1982)

Vítězslav Nezval [Czechoslavakia/ now Czech Republic] 1900-1958

Vítězslav Nezval was born on May 16, 1900 into a family of a village teacher in Šamikovice in Southern Moravia. His father had cultivated an interest in the arts and had traveled long distances to see important exhibitions. He was especially involved with music and his teacher was the composer Leoš Janáček. Nezval's grand-uncle was an eccentric toolmaker and telegraph clerk, a man who knew the world and spoke several languages—"half scientist, half poet," Nezval would later describe him. The young boy's life was profoundly marked by these two men but also by the village culture, close to nature, and the vocabulary of those who  worked the soil. In 1911 Nezval entered the gymnasium in Trebic, where he also learned piano and began composing music. From 1916 on he was systematically reading and writing his first poetry. In March of 1918 he as drafted into the first world war, but he was sent home soon thereafter for partly real and partly simulated illnesses.

With the war over, in the fall of 1919 Nezval moved to Prague and started studying philosophy at Charles University. This was the time when a newly formed Czechoslovakia (under its philosopher-president Thomas Masaryk) was emerging as the first real and socially oriented democracy in central Europe, and the question of its further political and economic direction was in contention. Like most other Czech artists and intellectuals, Nezval veered toward the left and in 1924 became a member of the Communist Party. As with others also—not only in Prague but throughout Europe—political revolution had its artistic counterpart, and from 1922 on, Nezval allied himself with the "Nine Powers" *(Devetsil)*, a collective of poets and artists that included among its core figures Jindrich Styrsky, Jaroslav Seifert, Karel Teige, Frantisek Halas, and Toyen (Marie Germinova). Written before his twenty-second birthday, Nezval's long poem, *The Remarakble Magician,* was included in the group's "Revolutionary Collections," a series of books of essays, poems, and manifestos, that accompanied the founding of a new "poetism" as the principal Czech avant-garde movement.

Nezval dated his own "discovery of Poetism" from 1923. As a program and a poetics—developed by Nezval and Teige in the latter's 1924 *Poetist Manifesto* (contemporary with André Breton's *Manifesto of Surrealism*)—Poetism set itself against "literary poetry" and proposed "a new art which will cease to be art." In a tension shared by other movements of the time and later, their "poetism" tilted between a rejection of "art" in the named of "a pure poetry... [within] a life [turned] into a magnificent entertainment" (Tiege) and a commitment to political and social struggle taking shape around a nascent and, for them, a still admired Soviet Union. Nezval would later rename the movement "realism" and later still would ally it for several years with the Surrealists of Paris.

In this way Nezval's public career moved between political and literary commitments and alliances. With the onset of the Great Depression of the 1920s and 30s he engaged directly in labor struggles—those in particular of striking Czech coal miners. In 1932 he attended the first Congress of Soviet Writers in Moscow, and in the same year he made an extensive and for him a transformative trip to Italy and to France, where he met with the leaders of the French avant-garde: Breton, Eluard, Péret, Aragon. At the same time his recognition as a poet—the central figure of the new Czech poetry—continued to grow. He received the prestigious State Prize for poetry in 1934 and donated the entire sum to a fund for helping refugees from Nazi Germany.

Nezval's meeting with the French poets and his continuing involvement with Surrealism had a kind of inevitability about it. As early as 1924 the event and content of Breton's Surrealist Manifesto of that year (along with that of Yvan Goll) had been disseminated in Prague. From the early 1920s on, Nezval's connection as writer and dramaturge with Jinrich Honzl's Liberated Theater involved him in the presentation and translation of works by Apollinaire, Jarry, Soupault, and Breton, among others. The painters Syrsky and Toyen, both close to him, emigrated to France and entered actively into the Paris art scene. From 1928 to 1931 Styrsky, along with Karel Tiege, published a number of key articles concerning French Surrealism, and in 1931 three important shows of French avant-garde painting were organized in Prage (an internationally based *Poetry* '32 exhibition came shortly thereafter), with Nezval intimately involved in their planning and presentation.

It was only after Nezval's 1932 meeting with Breton, however, that a more formal collaboration was set in motion. Nezval came to the Surrealists' defense against attacks by the Russian writer Ilya Ehrenburg, and in 1934 eleven writers, poets and painters in Prague, published a manifesto, written largely by Nezval and Teige, in which they presented themselves as part of the international surrealist movement and a proclamation of a decision to form a Czech Surrealist group.

The alliance between Prague and Paris led to a period of heightened activity on the Czech side: new books and magazines, art exhibitions, visits from Breton and Eluard and others, the establishment of the Surrealist-oriented New Theater with its productions of Breton and Aragon's *The Treasury of Jesuits* and Nezval's *The Oracle of Delphi*. With its balancing act of poetry and political absolutes, however, the Czech group, much like is Parisian prototype, began quickly to come apart. In 1938, while Europe was heading into new war, Nezval issued a proclamation dissolving the movement, which for a year or so continued existence under Teige and a group of interested young intellectuals and artists.

For Nezval the war period was a time of withdrawal and holding back. When the Germans took control of Czechoslovakia in March of 1939, he was not persuaded to leave the country, although arrangements had been made for him to do so. Most of his books were forbidden as "degenerate art," and he turned his attention to painting and to the writing of plays, most notably *Manon Lescaut,* based on Prévost's famous eighteenth century novel. In 1944 Nezval was arrested by Germans but was released soon thereafter.

After the liberation in 1945, Nezval returned to poetry and to increasingly recognized publication, though rarely with the avant-garde thrust of his earlier work. For a while he was the director of the film section of the Information and Culture Ministry in Prague, and after the

Communist takeover in 1948 he received a number of official prizes and considerable govern-
mental support. His political affinities and international stature made him a prominent
member of that network of tolerated avant-gardists/poet-heroes that included Neruda,
Brecht, Picasso, Hikmet, Eluard, and Tzara, some of whom he shared pro-forma hymns to
Stalin in the early postwar years. In 1945 he again traveled to France, this time to meet Picasso
and to see the French premier of his play *Today the Sun Is Setting on Atlantis*. But by then he
had experienced his first heart attack and he had the sense that death was closing in on him.

The last years of Nezval's life were a time of frenetic activity—publishing poems, essays,
and copious translations of world literature. Nezval died on April 6, 1958.

—JEROME ROTHENBERG AND MILOS SOVAK

BOOKS OF POETRY:

Most (Brno: Bedřich Kočí, 1922); *Pantomina* (Prague: Ústřední studentské knihkupectví
nakladatelství, 1924); *Diabolo* (Prague: Vaněk & Votava, 1926); *Karneval* (Prague: Jan Fromek,
1926); *Menší růžová zahrada* (Prague: Jan Fromek, 1926); *Akrobat* (Prague: Rudolf Škeřík,
1927); *Blíženci* (Prague: Rozmach, 1927); *Edison* (Prague: Rudolf Škeřík, 1928); *Hra v kostky*
(Prague: Rudolf Škeřík, 1929); *Básně noci* (Prague: Aventinum, 1930); *Jan ve smutku* (Prague:
Bohumil Janda, 1930); *Posedlost* (Prague: Bohumil Janda, 1930); *Snídaně v trávě* (Prague:
Aventinum, 1930); *Skleněný havelok* (Prague: František Borový, 1932); *Zpáteční lístek* (Prague:
František Borový, 1933); *Sbohem a šáteček* (Prague: František Borový, 1934); *Žena v množném
čísle* (Prague: František Borový, 1936); *Praha s prsty deště* (Prague:František Borový, 1936);
Absolutní hrobař. Básně 1937 (Prague: František Borový, 1937); *Historický obraz* (Prague:
František F. Müller, 1939; expanded edition, Prague: Melantrich, 1945); *Pět minut za městem*
(Prague: František Borový, 1940); *Stalin* (Prague: Československý spisovatel, 1949); *Zpěv míru*
(Prague: Československý spisovatel, 1950); *Chrpy a měta* (Prague: Československý spisovatel,
1955); *Dílo Vítězslava Nezvala*, (30 vols.) (Prague: Československý spisovatel, 1950-1990)

ENGLISH LANGUAGE TRANSLATIONS:

Song of Peace, trans. by Jack Lindsay and Stephen Jolly (London: Fore, 1951); in *Three Czech
Poets: Vítězslav Nezval, Antonín Bartušek, Josef Hanzlík* (Harmondsworth, United Kingdom:
Penguin, 1971); *Antilyrik and Other Poems*, trans. by Jerome Rothenberg and Milos Sovak (Los
Angeles: Green Integer, 2001); *Alphabet*, trans. by Jindrich Toman and Matthew S. Witkovsky
(Ann Arbor: Michigan Slavic Publications, 2001).

Novel

It's on the gazes of the women
that it flickers   in the length of mirrors
an indigo adventure
mixes with the midday sleep of soda water breaking free
extinguishing the evening

A cigarette draws off a day that's past
a memory in a box with the geraniums of summer
fragrance fading as the garbage truck rolls past

So when I paint these eyes
it's an enormous still life   these eyelasses brushing
the down comforter on which the setting sun
projects a a tree top as a cypress idyll

Farewell the grimace from the far side of the lawn
where some great game bird starts up the evening show
but stops short sobbing into her black pearls
in the backwash of a kiss that strips you bare

& now I see her standing naked
where the cafe mirrors multiply her image
until it lets me fall asleep
& I forget my indigo deception

An exchange of gazes
buzzes now like poisons
above the ranunculus's sweet inebriations
united by an icy chandelier

Then there's a letter slipped into a magazine
& later taken out
that I'm now burning in this ash tray

Or there's a handkerchief that some one dropped
and that a waiter picked up eyes fixed on his shoes

And the next day footsteps marking time
were entering the trolley   an exchange of greetings
our first rendezvous

What rotten luck
a rainy day three hours talking on the bathhouse colonnade
the indigo dissolved is dying out
in the thin blue opening between the little clouds

Loud ticking of a watch a sash that rustles like a snake's tongue
ironic crunch of chocolates a cry emitted where the makeup doesn't
    take
a frayed bouquet of peonies small boudoirs of the sun

Pieces of luggage left on desolation highway
deprived of combs and handkerchiefs and photographs and letters
an offhanded wave adieu
out on the platform reading destination: moon
damp cold & disenchanted

Until one day in an elevator without memories
a meeting with a flash of ostrich feathers on a little blonde
sparks a renewal of the poet's chessboard
& oh the games I play on it oh darkest night

—*Translated from the Czech by Jerome Rothenberg and Milos Sovak*

Shirt

[PREAMBLE]

How do they seize me these strange beings with no names
All their history as simple as Gibraltar
Bastards of reality & air who wander over Africa
The angelus clangs out
......

On one of those steamy nights the end of June in 1935
I walked past the Luxembourg Garden
It was just striking midnight
& the streets were empty
With the emptiness of moving vans
Deserted like Ash Wednesday
& I thought of nothing

Had no wishes
No I wished for nothing rushed to nowhere
Nothing weighed on me
Like a man sans memory I walked and walked
A man & yes like a box
The way old men walk who no longer need to sleep

I still don't know what caught me maybe my own sigh
The trees out in the garden filling with white bandages
I looked back at those paper bindings
Over an iron hedge
Could I have been singing as I walked?
Just singing
& Paris sold off like a slave
Convulsed & crazy
Paris with your bridges made into your chains
Prague, Paris, Leningrad and all the cities
                    I have ever walked thru
Now I see a herd of women bound with ropes
The glow in drowning them the sky still free
Like bracelets that a crowd is rushing over
Oh you gates you bridges
Of the one and only city that I see
A city cut thru by the Seine & Neva
by the Moldau
& a brook where peasant women wash their clothes
The brook I live by

& windows
Thru the first a statue comes in from the Place du Pantheon
The next looks over the Charles Bridge
Thru the third I'm staring down the Nevsky Prospect
& still more windows

How I love the grocer's paper cones
With secrets that lie too deep
That they remind me of an empty chamber
With its heaps & heaps of shirts
A shaft that holds the common grave of nameless women
I know a forest with its broadleafed burdock
                    under which a girl's breasts' hidden
And a tin cross too & these white hands
A sofa stuffed with gauze that reeks of antiseptic

Who are you woman like a sewing machine I stare at
Like the Boulevard Montparnasse that self-same evening
When I was sitting down outside the Café Dôme
And studying the frieze on that one building there
     five storeys up
I thought that it was snowing
In my mind I took part in the final new year's eve
                    of the 19th century before it ended
Under a tree filled up with songs a carriage waited
In vain I tried to find the house the sewing machine inside
                its shuttle that held a thread I longed to have
Then walked back to the Luxembourg again
The wonder of those gardeners who care so for their trees
                        they wrap the fruit in little sacks
Like you who cover up your bare breasts with a shirt
As beautiful as a water pail turned over in a house of mourning
As beautiful as a needle in a birch bark with the year and date
     stitched in
As beautiful as a poppy head that's shaken by a bell
As beautiful as a shoe out in a flood floats past a window with an oil
     lamp
As beautiful as a wooden stake on which a butterfly is resting
As beautiful as a baked apple in the snow
As beautiful as a bedboard struck by lightning
As beautiful as a wet rag in a fire
As beautiful as a loaf of bread at midnight on the pavement
As beautiful as a button on a cloister wall
As beautiful as a treasure in a pot of flowers
As beautiful as a psychic's table and the words writ on the gate
As beautiful as a garland in a shooting gallery
As beautiful as a scissors snipping off a candlewick
As beautiful as a tear inside the eye
As beautiful as a the hairwheel of a clock inside a mare's ear
As beautiful as a diamond in a condotierre's rifle
As beautiful as teeth marks on an apple
As beautiful as the trees in the Luxembourg Garden
          the trees wrapped in white linen
               stiff with starch

—Translated from the Czech by Jerome Rothenberg and Milos Sovak

The Heart of the Musical Clock

1

Someday to have gone that far

to slip the white glove off

your eye fixed on that one spot on the ring

reality in motion colors sounds & smells

the clock in motion too but different

but different too from science

& from buying a new tie & looking all around you

but different too from thinking hard about it

THIS IS THE HEART OF THE MUSICAL CLOCK

2

In the end the upholsterer will have to be invited

at dusk the gardener lights the lights in the asparagus

& in the rosy raspberries a caterpillar's sleeping

DON'T HAVE NO TIME FOR WEEPING

Oh that fantastic doll in her green furs

3

There was that Japanese picture you once gave me

I lost it somewhere in a crush of people

there isn't any need to go that far for it

have you observed the laces on the bosoms of your lady friends?

that's what poetry is all about

4

A bird landed in the roses & broke its wing

once we could all learn something from these birds

but the bird landed in the bushes broke its wing & now says nothing

listening to the music of the wingless flugelhorn

5

Oh you pink watermills

a star fell in the clock & now it spins around!

let's go & wind up all those stars

whenever somebody betrays you

then it's time to fly in closer

Creole women back in Buenos Aires shining on the promenade

up there in the airplane

& in the pocket mirror

6

A butterfly has settled in a box

it was the butterflies pinned down we most regretted

but you were pinning words down with a dagger

I pressed the letter to my heart

& died

7

In the calendar it says the month of May

oh all you sixteen year old boys & twenty-seven year old women

in the calendar it says the month of May

& you there with a head & hands & legs

So I would change into a kiss a word a smell

would dissipate & vanish

like a dandelion

8

The windmill of the seasons

A summer night of violets & fireworks out in the little garden

Spring serenades you on a sugary guitar　　　With autumn there are walks & walkers

a nickelodeon plunks on all morning　　　an English park complete with fountain

In winter best of all (oh yes) to be a fan held by a lady muse

9

Windmill of love & the four comers

On the night stand Poudre Inconnu

In the Chinese silk a charm　　　　The red handkerchief conceals a dreadful

as of the almond tree　　　　　　　　　　　　　dagger

Southlands of love the Oranges the mouths the lemons

10

Karel Teige

What is the most beautiful thing inside the coffee house?

The red white flowers on the terrace across the way

11

Mikado
on the throne
is having a good time

The little glove all ready for the duel

A shoe hunting for glances like a mirror

This is the portrait of a lady in pastel

12
MAGAZINES

Some magazines look like the map of Oceania

what will my magazine named *Siren* look like?

13
THE GLANCES

Love is running along a line of lemon fizzes

the sparkling acrobatics of these eyes

oh you my sweetest bonbons

where does this fun & games express train run to?

from eye to eye into your green arcadia

the snow is interlaced with pink adornments

& maybe best of all a super ice cream

oh stay asleep my little vermin

oh you my cardinal stay fast asleep

14
AN EVENT

First we thought it was a secret sign

it could have been a MENU

only it was a calendar

above it there a burnt-out bulb was hanging

until an absolutely white man sauntered by

a woman with her face completely white

oh yes it only was a calendar

21

I don't remember the moon any more

ostensibly it didn't shine

ostensibly it was the new moon

15

Those incredibly small wives are our real heroes

relentlessly they call you on the phone

oh in your heart the bell plays games with you forever

each one of them gets on & screams HELLO!

lays the receiver down

& keeps you on hold until you die

16

GLOBE

GLOBE   - light

GLOBE   - bearer

GLOBE   - worm

GLOBE   - star

GLOBE   - gloom

GLOBE   - trotter

GLOBE

17

Someday to have gone that far

to cast aside your weary civilization

so all realities will glow in ultraviolet

but 17 poems will still be something different

& different too from what you first intended

from thinking hard & long to write a poem

THIS IS THE HEART OF THE MUSICAL CLOCK

A Duel

When she sent forth her fingers like a swarm of birds
Into the beard hairs of a man bowed down like barley
Her back started to pour down like rain
Over her buttocks   flowed like a bidet
An uneven fight it was
Old man & statue slugged it out
Ending with three swipes & a bloody dagger
But the killer
Falling to earth before his victim did
Eyes shut tight could see wild poppies
Which would scorch his beard with fire
Of a never gratified desire

—Translated from the Czech by Jerome Rothenberg and Milos Sovak

PERMISSIONS

Nishiwaki Junzaburō
1859-1945

Born of a well established family in Niigata, Nishiwaki first aspired to become a painter. He studied economics at Keiō University in Tokyo. During this period, he read extensively, particularly in foreign languages, and began writing his own work in Latin, French and English. Indeed, throughout his life, Nishiwaki often avoided the conventional use of his mother tongue, preferring instead to write for European readers.

His first two books, *Spectrum,* published in England in 1925 and *Poems Barbarous,* published in Tokyo in 1930, were collections of English poems. Even his Japanese poems sounded, to the Japanese ear, as foreign. His 1933 collection, *Ambarvalia* referred to a Roman agricultural rite, and several of his poems were influenced by Western works such as *The Waste Land* and *Ulysses.*

Yet, for all of its European associations, Nishiwaki's poetry is extremely grounded in place names and nature that is distinctly Japanese. With his surrealist-like passages and the juxtaposition of images, moreover, he revolutionized modern Japanese poetry. In *Tabibito kaerazu* (1947), he returned to more Eastern traditions, using forms such as the renga and other devices more common to Japanese writing. *Kindai no gūwa* (1953, The Modern Fable) is one of his greatest books. In this he creates a kind of discourse between East and West, between the ancient and the modern, and between concretism and abstraction. His later works moved even more in the direction of Joyce and other radical experimenters. He died in 1982.

BOOKS OF POETRY:

Spectrum, 1925; *Poems Barbarous,* 1930; *Ambarvalia* (Tokyo: Shii no Ki Sha 1933; revised Tokyo: Tokyo Shuppan Sha, 1947); *Tabibito kaerazu* (Tokyo: Tokyo Shuppan Sha, 1947); *Kindai no gūwa* (Tokyo: Sōgensha, 1953); *Andoromeda* (Tokyo: Toraiton Sha, 1955) [a revision of part of his book of 1930]; *Daisan no shinwa* (Tokyo: Tokyo Sōgensha, 1956); *Ushinaware toki* (Tokyo: Seiji Kōron Sha, 1960); *Hōjō no megami* (Tokyo: Sinchōsha, 1962); *Eterunaitasu* (Tokyo: Sinchōsha, 1962); *Hōseki no nemuri* (Tokyo: Chikuma Shobō, 1963); *Raiki* (Tokyo: Chikuma Shobō, 1967); *Jōka* (Tokyo: Chikuma Shobō, 1969); *Rokumon* (Tokyo: Chikuma Shobō, 1970); *Jinrui* (Tokyo: Chikuma Shobō, 1979)

Cup's Primitivism

Along the riverbank where daphnes bloom
and shine,
passing by an angel who has an apple and a saber,
a blond boy runs,
holding firmly between his fingers
a fish called *red-belly*
above its milk-light eyes.
The golden dream warps.

—*Translated from the Japanese by Hiroaki Sato*

(from *Ambarvalia*, 1933)

A Man Who Reads Omeros

The daybreak and the twilight, quietly,
like the two sides of a gold coin,
passed through a tamarind,
and come every day to his throat.
In those days he boarded at a dyer's
on the second floor and read *Omeros*.
In those days he had a coral pipe
with a picture of pansies.
The Galileans all laughed (Your pipe
looks like a girl's letter or
a Byzantine romane — *Uuee*).
But its phosphorescent smoke circles
cockscomb bloom,
and the goddess' nose and hips.

—*Translated from the Japanese by Hiroaki Sato*

(from *Ambarvalia*, 1933)

The Modern Fable

The fable at the end of April is linear.
On the peninsula the bronze wheat and aloe-green rape
were rusted like the willowy woman's robe.
One thinks; therefore, existence ceases to be.
Man's existence is after death.
When one ceases to be human one merges
with greatest existence. For now
I don't want to talk a lot.
It's simply that with the people in the poppy house
with the people doing metaphysical mythology
I take a hot bath in Ochiai where mustard grows.
I think secretly of Andromeda.
In the house beyond the willowy woman, lying on her side,
plays *go* with a woman.
She ponders, her hand stuck out of the front of her robe.
We philosophers gathered before the broken water wheel
and holding azalea and sweet flag in our hands
had a photo taken, had another hot bath
served ourselves an arrowhead-like liquor
and immersed all night in geometrical thoughts.
I think of a friend of the days
when we talked about Beddoes' suicide theory
as we climbed the Dōgenzaka, and also thinking
about the white-haired Einstein walking
in an American village, I cannot sleep.
I run along the Nekko river alone.
Early in the morning I walk the white road to an inn at Seko.
A damson tree with white blossoms stands
crooked at the roadside. I turn toward a bush warbler's
song and see blossoms of mountain cherries already fallen.
Pale violets clinging to rocks   cattails
dropped in great masses in the mist.
My hair has turned badger-gray.
All of a sudden an Ophelian thought:
wild strawberry   vetch buttercups wild roses
violets I picked

I hold this full bouquet with a pencil in my hand
for the willowy woman for the never-ending love
for a curses of Pascal's and Rilke's women
and for this water spirit.

—*Translated from the Japanese by Hiroaki Sato*

(from *Kindai no gūwa*, 1953)

The Winter Day

What age was it when they made this garden?
There aren't many
who walk this road
but in this valley where giant elms
twist their branches into the sky
I pick the seeds of wild roses
for your gourd.
Liquor may be exhausted but dreams spurt on endlessly.
Dangling a string of empty cups from my forefinger
brows raised and like a breeze
I go with a man to the blue sea
On a day like this the biologist
wearing the pear-colored tie
tells heartless stories
of sea anemones and wild grapes.
In the moonlight that Neptune casts
in weather like this, quite unseen
another god of *gonzui*
splits solemnly.
Thus imagining gaudy matters
smoking my hackberry pipe
I ran toward the Meguro station to see the winter festival.
Near the station at a house called Scipio
an old woman was playing the flute
carousing.
From behind me a boy pulled at my mantle dyed purplish indigo
with grass green lining.
"Mackerel pike and chestnuts are out of season but would you
please honor us by dropping in
my master says.

Mr. Socrates is here too."
This is the beginning of
Plato's *Republic.*

—*Translated from the Japanese by Hiroaki Sato*

(from *Kindai no gūwa*, 1953)

Winter Day

In the desolate season
I roamed
the horizon of the endless mind
and strayed into a village
a hawthorn hedge set around it.
A vagabond cooks dog meat on a fire
from which a purple cloud flows away.
The man who sang at summer's end the song of roses
grieves over this heart's ruination.
The seed collector, the bulbul, does not talk.
I will study in this village, with a lamp on
"Study like Milton"
whispers an angel like a university president.
And yet I ended up playing chess with a hunter and a fisherman
until the bush put on pear-like blossoms.
Now that I've lost everything
I'd like to consecrate this evening
to the person who circles the hedge
playing with butterflies
to the kingfisher and the man that stray in
to the eternal woman
to this winter day
putting in a cup with a long handle like a lofty tower
the haws and the tears.

—*Translated from the Japanese by Hiroaki Sato*

(from *Kindai no gūwa*, 1953)

Atalanta's Calydon

the flash of the day one discovers
tigers among the stones of
the garden where *oniyuri* bloom
one discovers lilies among roses
ah this lovely summer afternoon
among wild roses of the hedge
the Dorian puts on his head a scarlet-lacquered
wooden cup and dances
sufferings of mankind
under the snow
a scouring rush
a woman comes up the stone steps
to play chess
through the rear gate

the Fukazawa matron
all her life in a faded pink waist-cloth
brazen as a wolf
for her cheekbones
I give her a plate Picasso made

spring comes to Snow Woman's garden
I give the woman
who wore purple stockings while alive
Tales of Ise translated into Arabian

moss
stone
apple
autumn haze
black fruit of trifoliate orange
gust of dust
dream's sufferings
the Yase road reminds one of past and present
fruit of wild rose sag over a rock
to the old person, a woman,
who had *matsutake* for a souvenir
a city student used a startling word
soon a snowy night
boars wreck the radish garden

bulbuls eat nandin seeds
but all day long drinking from a gourd
I talked with Mr. Sakurai about plums
then while I sit by a foot-warmer
and read Ptolemy's astronomical book
jagged yellow flowers bloom
from bitter roots by the Yase road
a blue-green snake shiny with rain
coils around a hawthorn tree
the philosophy of rose and lily comes into being
rose fragrance wafts over narcissus
man smells of chrysanthemum
when man discards vegetable relations
does he become like a wire
self and self
self and wild rose
self and lover
self and God
self and eternity
Gourmont sticks out his tongue in the curtain
self as a wild rose
lover as a wild rose
eternity as a wild rose

Picasso the man
discovers a boy in a plate
discovers a plate in a boy
discovers man in a wild rose
a wild rose in man
love of wild rose is
the wild rose's emotion in man
man as a wild rose
wild rose as man
life has split into wild rose and man
but still its memory stains
the marriage between wild rose and man
looking in this hedge
a woman, her garden

—*Translated from the Japanese by Hiroaki Sato*

(from *Kindai no gūwa*, 1953)

Sorrow

Over the granite
spring has come
in the mountain depts of Jōshū
plum blossoms white
about the 20th of March.
on my way from funeral rites
I hurry toward the capital
the dead person's laughing
born of a rose
behind trumpet lilies
now I can only read Aesop's *Fables*
except I shouldn't read those sermons
there's the wonderful pastoral tragedy
to the greatness of that nameless
illustrator I consecrate carnations   mimosa
freesia   violets
here's a man in a triangular hood,
in briefs, wearing
a dagger, fishing,
the costume of which ethnic group is this
neither a Greek nor a Malay
that I should have never
thought about it before
it's a costume for a children's book
by an English illustrator during the Ansei era
harvesting wheat with a sickle like a crescent
and surprising skylarks
a man and a bass talking
a fox and a stork stand talking
vagabonds and travelers loitering
pricked by a thorn in a hedge
bleeding
wasp   locus   ant   water jar
wind   sun   grapes   adder
ancient oak   drowning child
a tower looking distorted in the distance

—*Translated from the Japanese by Hiroaki Sato*

(from *Kindai no gūwa*, 1953)

Stripping of Iphigenia

1

came:
color of hawthorn,
lilac of lilac,
blonde of hair,
the masculine woman

gasoline's crystal
Picasso's
metamorphosis, that line
weak-kneedly becomes a rose

2

head and arms
missing
the mass of stone, the dent
on its ass, its history
the fluffly bundle of blonde hair
ends in the middle
sticks to the back and remains
the severed Babylonian goddess' lust
thought's emotion
comes from nowhere
comes a pitiful summer
as a bee comes to grape flowers

3

haw
scraping the window
the acorn cup and thorns
"I've never been in love
but a man's voice and form
have been haunting me for the last two days"

the auntie who wrote me this
is worried

—Translated from the Japanese by Hiroaki Sato

(from *Kindai no gūwa,* 1953)

Bowls

Under the lacquer-
growing bank
the woodcarver turns his wheel
enshrines a woman the white mountain goddess
and loves the demon's ladle
that grows in the oak's thighs.
The man drinks cheap tea in his office
and keeps skylarks and sparrows
in his house; his summer
by hell time is noon.
This man of sorrows
in the shadow
mottled
like grouse plumage
quietly
carves bowls for
Americans
to pile salads in.
Ladles too.

Until an arrow
stabs the heart,
wheel,
turn quietly.
The tube
that loiters
around the wood spirit
tries to grow wings
and fly away
toward the light on the horizon.
The sound of the Wood Star
tickles the navel

of a tired man
on the bridge.
Man's last laughter
reaches the modern man
walking on the riverbed.
This protruding navel's
last laugh
reaches
both the stone clouded with reed warblers' shit
and the acacia thorns.
The god's lone laugh
boils his last tea
for the disappointed tired man
leaning on the bridge rail.
This god's blessing,
this last joy
of man.

—Translated from the Japanese by Hiroaki Sato

(from *Hōseki no nemuri*, 1963)

PERMISSIONS

"Cup's Primitivism," "A Man Who Reads Omeros," "The Modern Fable," "The Winter Day,"
"Winter Day," "Atalanta's Calydon," "Sorrow," "Stripping of Iphigenia," and "Bowls"
Reprinted from *The Modern Fable* (manuscript), trans. by Hiroaki Sato, ©Hiroaki Sato, 2000.
Reprinted by permission Hiroaki Sato and Green Integer.

Octavio Paz [Mexico]
1914-1998

Born in Mexico City, the son of a lawyer, Octavio Paz was educated at National Autonomous University of Mexico, which he attended from 1932-1937. Paz began writing poetry in 1933, with the publication of *Luna silvestre,* and over the years established himself as the major Mexican poet and essayist. He was awarded the Nobel Prize for literature in 1990.

Paz's work is highly varied, but one of the major elements of his writing is a tendency to push poetry into prose so that the differentiation between the two is nearly indistingable. This is particularly so of *El mono gramático (The Monkey Grammarian),* published in 1974, which grew out of Paz's desire to publish a text which would intersect poetry, narrative, and essay. Other texts, such as *Hijos del Aire* and *Renga* are written in more than one language. Behind this is a constant attempt in his work of searching for the international community, of striving for a universality in his work that yet acknowledges the world's diversity.

Among his other books of poetry are *¿Aguila o sol?* (1951), *Piedra de sol* (1957), *Blanco* (1967), and *Vuelta* (1971). He also translated William Carlos Williams, Guillaume Apollinaire, and numerous other poets into Spanish.

The critic Ronald Christ has summarized Paz's career: "By contraries…, by polarities and divergences converging in a rhetoric of opposites, Paz established himself as a brilliant stylist balancing the tension of East and West, art and criticism, the many and the one in the figures of his writing. Paz is thus not only a great writer; he is also an indispensable corrective to our cultural tradition and a critic in the highest sense in which he himself uses the word."

BOOKS OF POETRY:

Luna silvestre (Mexico City: Fábula, 1933); *¡No pasarán!* (Mexico City: Simbad, 1936); *Raíz del hombre* (Mexico City: Simbad, 1937); *Bajo tu clara sombra y otros poems sobre España* (Valencia: Españolas, 1937, revised ed. Valencia: Tierra Nueva, 1941); *Entre la piedra y la flor* (Mexico City: Nueva Voz, 1938); *A la orilla del mundo y Primer día; Bajo tu clara somba; Raíz del hombre; Noche de resurreccions* (Mexico City: Ars, 1942); *Libertad bajo palabra* (Mexico City: Tezontle, 1949); *¿Aguila o sol?* (Mexico City: Tezontle, 1951); *Semillas para un himno* (Mexico City: Tezontle, 1954); *Piedra de sol* (Mexico City: Tezontle, 1957); *La estación violenta* (Mexico City: Fondo de Cultura Económica, 1958); *Agua y viento* (Bogotá: Ediciones Mito, 1959); *Libertad bajo palabra: Obra poética, 1935-1959* (Mexico City: Fondo de Cultura

Económica, 1960; revised ed., 1968); *Salamandra* (1959-1951) (Mexico City: J. Mortiz, 1962); *Viento entero* (Delhi: Caxton, 1965); *Blanco* (Mexico City: J. Moritz, 1967); *Disco visuales* (Mexico City: Era, 1968); *Ladera este (1962-1968)* (Mexico City: J. Moritz, 1969); *La centena* (Poemas: 1935-1968) (Barcelona: Seix Barral, 1969); *Topoemas* (Mexico City: Era, 1971); *Vuelta* (Mexico City: El Mendrugo, 1971/Barcelona: Seix Barral, 1976); *Renga* [with Jacques Roubaud, Edoardo Sanguinetti, and Charles Tomlinson] (Mexico City: J. Mortiz, 1972); *Pasado en claro* (Mexico City: Fondo de Cultura Económica, 1975); *Air Born/Hijos del aire* [with Charles Tomlinson] (Mexico City: Pescador, 1979); *Poemas (1935-1975)* (Barcelona: Seix Barral, 1979); *Octavio Paz: Poemas recientes* (Institución Cultural de Cantabria de la Diputación Provincial de Santander, 1981)

BOOKS IN ENGLISH:

Selected Poems of Octavio Paz, trans. by Muriel Rukeyser (Bloomington: Indiana University Press, 1963); *Sun Stone/Piedra de sol,* trans. by Muriel Rukeyser (New York: New Directions, 1963); *Sun-Stone,* trans. by Peter Miller (Toronto: Contact, 1963); *Sun Stone,* trans. by Donald Gardner (New York: Cosmos, 1969); *Eagle or Sun?* trans. by Eliot Weinburger (New York: October House, 1970/New York: New Directions, 1976); *Configurations* (contains Sun Stone, Blanco, and selections from Salamadra and Ladera este), trans. by G. Aroul and others (New York: New Directions 1971); *Renga: A Chain of Poems* (New York: Braziller 1972); *Early Poems: 1935-1955,* trans. by Muriel Rukeyser and others (New York: New Directions, 1973); *Blanco,* trans. by Eliot Weinberger (New York: The Press, 1974); *A Draft of Shadows and Other Poems,* trans. by Eliot Weinberger, Elizabeth Bishop and Mark Strand (New York: New Directions, 1979); *Selected Poems,* trans. by Charles Tomlinson and others (Harmonsworth, England: Penguin, 1979); *Selected Poems,* trans. by Eliot Weinberger (New York: New Directions, 1984); *Cuatro chopos/The Four Poplars,* trans. by Eliot Weinburger (New York: Center for Edition Works, 1985); [with Marie José Paz] *Figures & Figurations,* trans. by Eliot Weinberger (New York: New Directions, 2002).

Night Walk

Night draws from its body one hour after another. Each different, each solemn. Grapes, figs, sweet drops of quiet blackness. Fountains: bodies. Wind plays the piano among the stones of the ruined garden. The lighthouse stretches its neck, turns, goes out, cries out. Crystals a thought dims, softness, invitations: night, immense and shining leaf plucked from the invisible tree that grows at the center of the world.

Around the corner, Apparitions: the girl who becomes a pile of withered leaves if you touch her; the stranger who pulls off his mask and remains faceless, fixedly staring at you; the ballerina who spins on the point of a scream; the who goes here?, the who are you?, the where am I?; the girl who moves like a murmur of birds; the great tower destroyed by inconclusive thought, open to the sky like a poem split in two... No, none of these is the one you wait for, the sleeper who waits for you in the folds of her dream.

Around the corner, Plants end and stones begin. There is nothing, nothing you can give the desert, not a drop of water, not a drop of blood. You move with bandaged eyes through corridors, plazas, alleys where three vile stars conspire. The river speaks softly. To your left, to your right, ahead, behind: whispers and cruel laughter. The monologue traps you at every step with its exclamations, its question marks, its noble sentiments, its dots over the i's in the middle of a kiss, its mill of laments, its repertory of broken mirrors. Go on: there's nothing you can say to yourself.

—*Translated from the Spanish by Eliot Weinberger*

(from *¿Águila o Sol?*, 1951)

Curse

Tonight I invoked all the powers. No one answered. I walked streets, crossed plazas, knocked on doors, smashed mirrors. My shadow deserted, memories abandoned me.

(Memory is not what we remember, but that which remembers us. Memory is a present that never stops passing. It waits in hiding and suddenly grabs us with hands of smoke that never loosen their grip. It slips into our blood: he who we were is planted in us and throws us out. A thousand years ago, one afternoon when leaving school, I spat on my soul, and now my soul is that infamous place, the little square, the ash trees, the ocher wall, the endless afternoon in which I spit on my soul. A perpetual and irreparable present lives within us. That child pelted by stones, that female sex like a fascinating cleft, that adolescent who commands an army of birds to assault the sun, that tall crane with the small dinosaur head bending to devour a passer-by: at times they expel me from myself, they live within me, they live me. But not tonight.)

Why carve signs and names with a rusty knife on the bark of night? The first waves of morning erase all these tracks. Whom can I invoke at this hour, and against whom chant exorcisms? There is no one above nor below, no one behind the door, in the next room, outside the house. There is no one, there has never been anyone, there never will be anyone. There is no I. And the other, he who thinks me, does not think me tonight. He thinks another, he thinks himself. I am circled by a sea of sand and fear, covered with a growth of spiders. I travel through myself like a reptile between broken stones, mass of debris and bricks without history. The water of time drips slowly in this cracked hollow, cave where all the stiff words rot.

—*Translated from the Spanish by Eliot Weinberger*

(from *¿Águila o Sol?*, 1951)

Cypher

CIFRA= cipher
COMO = like
CALMA = calm
CERO= zero
COLMO = abundance

(from *Topoemas*, 1968)

The Petrifying Petrified

Deadland
           Shadeadland cactideous nopalopolis
bonéstony dushty mockedmire
                              empty socket
petrified fire
                  the sun did not drink the lake
the earth did not absorb it
                              the water did not vanish in the air
men were the executors of the dust
wind
           swirled in the cold bed of fire
wind
           chanted litanies of drought
in the tomb of water
                         wind
broken knife in the worn crater
                                   wind
saltpeter whisper

                   The sun
solaortasoul centrotal soldonage
                                 split
the word that came down in tongues of fire
                                         smashed
the account and the count of the years
the chant of the days
                           was a rain of scrap iron
slagheap of words
                      sand primers
crushed screams
                     hoofmuz zlebridlehar nessbit
whining waning Cains
                         Ables in rubble
partisan assassins
                      pagan pedagogues
slick crooks
               the woofs of the one-eyed dog
guide of the dead

                         lost
          in the coils of the Navel of the Moon

          Valley of Mexico
                         lips in eclipse
          lava slobber
                         Rage's rotten throne
          obstinate obsidian
                                   petrified
          petrifying
                    Rage
                         broken tower
          tall as a scream
                              smeared breasts
          tense brow
                         greendry bloodsnot
                                        Rage
          nailed in a wound
                              ragerazor gazeblade
          on a land of tines and spines

                         Circus of mountains
          theater of clouds
                              table of noon
          mat of the moon
                              garden of planets
          drum of rain
                         balcony of breezes
          seat of the sun
                         ball-game of the constellations
          Bursting images
                         impaled images
          the lopped hand leaps
                              the uprooted tongue leaps
          the sliced breasts leap
                              the guillotined penis
          over and over in the dust over and over
                                        in the couryard
          they trim the tree of blood
                              the intelligent tree

The dust of stuffed images
                              The Virgin
crown of snakes
                      The Flayed
The Felled-by-Arrows
                              The Crucified
The Hummingbird
                      winged spark
flowerbrand
                The Flame
who speaks with words of water
                                      Our Lady
breasts of wine and belly of bread
                                      oven
where the dead burn and the living bake
The Spider
                daughter of air
in her house of air
                              spins light
spins centuries and days
                              The Rabbit
wind
          carved in the mirror of the moon

                                      Images buried
          in the eye of the dog of the dead
                                      fallen
in the overgrown well of origins
                                              whirlwinds of reflections
in the stone theater of memory
                                      images
whirling in the circus of the empty eye
                                              ideas
of red brown green
                      swarms of flies
ideas ate the deities
                      deities
became ideas
                great bladders full of bile

the bladders burst
                    the idols exploded
putrefaction of the deities
                              the sanctuary was a dungheap
the dungheap a nursery
                         armed ideas sprouted
idealized ideodeities
                    sharpened syllogisms
cannibal deities
                    ideas idiotic as deities
rabid dogs
          dogs in love with their own vomit

We have dug up Rage
The amphitheater of the genital sun is a dungheap
The fountain of lunar water is a dungheap
The lovers' park is a dungheap
The library is a nest of killer rats
The university is a muck full of frogs
The altar is Chanfalla's swindle
The brains are stained with ink
The doctors dispute in a den of thieves
The businessmen
fast hands   slow thoughts
officiate in the graveyard
The dialecticians exalt the subtlety of the rope
The casuists sprinkle thugs with holy water
nursing violence with dogmatic milk
The idée fixe gets drunk with its opposite
The juggling ideologist
                         sharpener of sophisms
in his house of truncated quotations and assignations
plots Edens for industrious eunuchs
forest of gallows   paradise of cages
               Stained images
                spit on the origins
          future jailers   present leeches
          affront the living body of time
               We have dug up Rage

On the chest of Mexico
                    tablets written by the sun
stairway of the centuries
                    spiral terrace of wind
the disinterred dances
                    anger panting thirst
the blind in combat beneath the noon sun
                                    thirst panting anger
beating each other with rocks
                    the blind are beating each other
the men are crushing
                    the stones are crushing
within there is a water we drink
                    bitter water
water whetting thirst

                    Where is the other water?

—Translated from the Spanish by Eliot Weinberger

(from *Vuelta*, 1971)

Vasko Popa [Yugoslavia/ now Serbia and Montenegro] 1922-1991

Vasko Popa was born in Grebenac in the Banat district of Yugoslavia, now Serbia to a family of mixed Serbian and Romanian extraction. He studied literature at the universities of Vienna, Bucharest, and Belgrade, and received his degree in 1949. During World War II, he supported the partisans, and was arrested and imprisoned by the Nazis.

His first collection, *Kora* (Bark), was published in 1953, to a negative response by readers and critics unreceptive to Yugoslav modernization. His second book, *Nepočin-polje* (Unrest-Field) and subsequent titles, along with the work of Popa's friend Miodrag Pavlović, were major influences on Serbian contemporary writing. Beginning with concrete images, Popa's poetry functioned to create surreal narratives that had larger, abstract concepts as their goal. In that sense, Popa's affinity to the folk tradition is apparent, but his major influence is French surrealism, which renders his work highly experimental within the Serbian context.

Among his other titles are *Sporedno nebo* (1968, The Secondary Heaven), *Vučja so* (1975, Wolf Salt), and *Mala kutija* (The Little Box, 1970).

Popa came to the forefront of international poetry in 1970s, and traveled widely. He also edited anthologies, one of folk writing and another of Serbian humor.

BOOKS OF POETRY:

Kora (Belgrade: Novo pokolenje, 1953); *Nepočin-polje* (Novi Sad: Matica srpska, 1956); *Od zlata jabuka* (1958); *Pesme* (Belgrade: Srpska književna zadruga, 1965); *Sporedno nebo* (Belgrade: Prosveta, 1968); *Pesme* (Belgrade: Prosveta, 1968); *Pesme* (Novi Sad: Srpska književna zadruga, 1971); *Uspravna zemlja* (Belgrade: Vuk Karadžić, 1975); *Vučja so* (Belgrade: Vuk Karadžić, 1975); *Živo meso* (Belgrade: Vuk Karadžić, 1975); *Kuća nasred druma* (Belgrade: Vuk Karadžić, 1975); *Pesme* (Belgrade: BIGZ, 1978); *Rez* (Novi Sad: Vojvodjansk Akademija nauka i umetnosti, 1982); *Pesme* (Belgrade: Nolit, 1988); *Dela* (8 volumes) (Belgrade: Nolit, 1980-1981)

ENGLISH LANGUAGE TRANSLATIONS:

Selected Poems, trans. by Anne Pennington, introduction by Ted Hughes (Harmondsworth: Penguin, 1969): *The Little Box*, trans. by Charles Simic (Washington, D.C.: The Charioteer Press, 1970); *Earth Erect*, trans. by Anne Pennington (London: Anvil Press, 1973/Iowa City:

University of Iowa International Writing Program, 1973); *Collected Poems* 1943-1976, trans. by Anne Pennington, with an Introduction by Ted Hughes (Manchester: Carcanet, 1978/New York: Persea, 1979); *The Blackbird's Field: A Poem by Vasko Popa,* trans. by Anne Pennington (Oxford: Mid-Day Publications, 1979); *Homage to the Wolf: Selected Poems* 1956-1975, trans. by Charles Simic (Oberlin: The Field Translation Series, 1979; revised 1987); *The Golden Apple* (1980); in *The Horse Has Six Legs: An Anthology of Serbian Poetry,* trans. by Charles Simic (St. Paul, Minnesota: Graywolf Press, 1992); *Collected Poems,* trans. by Anne Pennington; revised and expanded by Francis R. Jones (London: Anvil Press, 1997).

Chestnut Tree

The street boozes away
All his green bank-notes
Whistles bells and horns
Weave nests in his crown
Spring prunes his fingers

He lives on the adventures
Of his unreachable roots
And on the wonderful memories
Of the surprise nights
When he vanishes from the streeet

Who knows where he goes

He'd get lost in a wood
But always by dawn
He's back in his place in the row

—*Translated from the Serbian by Anne Pennington*

(from *Kora,* 1953)

The Wedding

Each takes off his skin
Each uncovers his constellation
Which has never seen the night

Each fills his skin with stones
Each starts dancing with it
By the light of his own stars

He who doesn't stop until dawn
He who doesn't blink doesn't drop
He earns his skin

(This game is rarely played)

—*Translated from the Serbian by Anne Pennington*

(from *Nepoćin-polje*, 1956)

He

Some bite off the others'
Arm or leg or whatever

Take it between their teeth
Run off as quick as they can
Bury it in the earth

The others run in all directions
Sniff search sniff search
Turn up all the earth

If any are lucky enough to find their arm
Or leg or whatever
It's their turn to bite

The game goes on briskly

As long as there are arms
As long as there are legs
As long as there is anything whatever

—*Translated from the Serbian by Anne Pennington*

(from *Nepoćin-polje*, 1956)

Rose Thieves

Someone is a rose bush
The others are wind's daughters
The others are rose thieves

The rose thieves sneak up to the rose
One of them steals it
Hides it in his heart

The wind's daughters appear
See the picked beauty
And run after the thieves

They open their hearts one by one
In one they find a heart
In another so help me nothing

They open and open their chests
Until they find a heart
And in that heart a stolen rose

—Translated from the Serbian by Charles Simic

(from *Nepoćin-polje*, 1956)

The Tale About a Tale

Once upon a time there was a tale

It came to the end
Before its beginning
And begun
After its end

Its heroes entered it
After their death
And left it
Before their birth

Its heroes spoke
Of an earth of a heaven
They spoke a lot

Only they didn't say
What even they didn't know

That they were heroes in a tale

In a tale coming to the end
Before its beginning
And beginning
After its end

—*Translated from the Serbian by Charles Simic*

(from *Sporedno nebo,* 1968)

The Little Box

The little box gets her first teeth
And her little length
Little width little emptiness
And all the rest she has

The little box continues growing
The cupboard that she was inside
Is now inside her

And she grows bigger bigger bigger
Now the room is inside her
And the house and the city and the earth
And the world she was in before

The little box remembers her childhood
And by a great great longing
She becomes a little box again

Now in the little box
You have the whole world in miniature
You can easily put in a pocket
Easily steal it easily lose it

Take care of the little box

—*Translated from the Serbian by Charles Simic*

(from *Mala kutija,* 1970)

The Craftsmen of the Little Box

Don't open the little box
Heaven's hat will fall out of her

Don't close her for any reason
She'll bite the trouser-leg of eternity

Don't drop her on the earth
The sun's eggs will break inside her

Don't throw her in the air
Earth's bones will break inside her

Don't hold her in your hands
The dough of the stars will go sour inside her

What are you doing for God's sake
Don't let her get out of your sight

—Translated from the Serbian by Charles Simic

(from *Mala kutija,* 1970)

Last News About the Little Box

The little box that contains the world
Fell in love with herself
And conceived
Still another little box

The little box of the little box
Also fell in love with herself
And conceived
Still another little box

And so it went on forever

The world from the little box
Ought to be inside

The last offspring of the little box

But not one of the little boxes
Inside the little box in love with herself
Is the last one

Let's see you find the world now

—*Translated from the Serbian by Charles Simic*

(from *Mala kutija*, 1970)

Burning Shewolf

1

On the bottom of the sky
The shewolf lies

Body of living sparks
Overgrown with grass
And covered with sun's dust

In her breasts
Mountains rise threatening
And forgive as they lower themselves

Through her veins rivers thunder
In her eyes lakes flash

In her boundless heart
The ores melt with love
On seven stems of their fire

Before the first and last howl
Wolves play on her back
And live in her crystal womb

2

They cage the shewolf
In the earth's fire

Force her to build
Towers of smoke
Make bread out of coals

They flatten her with embers
And have her wash it down
With hot mercury milk

They force her to mate
With red-hot pokers
And rusty old drills

With her teen the shewolf reaches
The blonde braid of a star
And climbs back to the base of the sky

3

They catch the shewolf in steel traps
Sprung from horizon to horizon

Tear out her golden muzzle
And pluck the secret grasses
Between her thighs

They sick on her all-tie-up
Deadbeats and bloodhounds
To go ahead and rape her

Cut her up into pieces
And abandon her
To the carcass-eating tongs

With her severed tongue the shewolf
Scoops live water from the jaws of a cloud
And again becomes whole

4

The shewolf bathes herself in the blue
And washes away the ashes of dogs

On the bottom of a torrent
That runs down the stones of her motionless face
Lightnings spawn

In her wide-open jaw
The moon hides its ax during the day
The sun its knives at night

The beatings of her copper-heart
Quiet the barking distances
And lull to sleep the chirping air

In the ravines
Below her wooded eyebrows
The thunder means business

5

The shewolf stands on her back legs
At the base of the sky

She stands up together with wolves
Turned to stone in her womb

She stands up slowly
Between noon and midnight
Between two wolf lairs

Stands up with pain
Freeing from one lair her snout
And from the other her huge tail

She stands up with a salt-choked howl
From her dry throat

Stands up dying of thirst
Toward the clear point at the summit of the sky
The watering place of the long-tailed stars

—Translated from the Serbian by Charles Simic

(from *Vučja*, 1975)

PERMISSIONS

"Rose Thieves," "The Tale About a Tale," "Burning Shewolf," "The Little Box," "The Craftsmen of the Little Box," and "Last News About the Little Box"
Reprinted from *The Horse Has Six Legs: An Anthology of Serbian Poetry,* trans. by Charles Simic (St. Paul, Minnesota: Graywolf Press, 1992). Copyright ©1992 by Charles Simic. Reprinted by permission of Graywolf Press.

"Chestnut Tree," "The Wedding," and "He"
Reprinted from *Collected Poems,* trans. by Anne Pennington, revised and expanded by Francis R. Jones (London: Anvil Press, 1997). Copyright ©1953, 1956, 1965, 1968, 1972, 1975, 1981, 1988 by Vasko Popa. English language translation by Anne Pennington copyright ©1969, 1973, 1977 by Lady Margaret Hall, Oxford. Reprinted by permission of Anvil Press.

Yannis Ristsos [Greece]
1909-1990

Recognized as the foremost poet of the Greek polit-
ical left, Yannis Ristos is also one of the most pro-
ductive poets of the 20th century, with nearly 100
collections of poetry, as well as plays, essays and
other works, by the time of his death. He was also
an accomplished painter.

The youngest of four children, Ritsos was born
in Monemasiá, on the southwestern tipof Pelop-
enneosos. Despite his prolific output, his personal
life was filled with tragedy. At the age of twelve, his
older brother Dimitri died of tuberculosis; within
three months, his mother also died of the same dis-
ease, and he was striken with the disease and suf-
fered throughout his life. His father was sent to the asylum in Daphni for the mentally insane,
and Ritsos's sister, Loula, suffered from mental problems and was institutionalized in 1936.

From his late teens to his mid-twenties, Ritsos spent his time in and out of sanatoriums,
working when he was well as a dancer, a professional actor, and a poet. With the outbreak of
World War II, he joined the Greek Democratic Left, and followed its guerilla arm into retreat
before the Britsh troops in Northern Greece. In 1945 he headed the Popular Theatre of
Macedonia, a theater that exalted the actions of the partisans. During the Greek civil wars,
Ritsos was incarcerated as a prisoner in a number of concentration camps, and it was only
during the years from 1953 to 1967 that he was free to work full time on his great body of writ-
ing.

With the coup of Papadopoulous in 1967, and the junta attack on Greek liberties, Ritsos was
again arrested, imprisoned, and exiled on various islands, where he spent much of his time in
military hospitals fighting tuberculosis. Freed, he remained under house arrest until the stu-
dent revolt of 1974 which brought down the junta.

The last years of his life were spent between his home in Athens and his house on the island
of Samos, where his wife practiced medicine. He died in 1990.

BOOKS OF POETRY:

Trakert (Athens: Govostis, 1934); *Pyramides* (Athens: Govostis, 1935); *Epitafios* (Athens:
Rizospastis, 1936); *To tragoudi tes adelfis mou* (Athens: Govostis, 1937); *Earini Symfonia*
(Athens: Govostis, 1938); *To emvatiro tou okeanou* (Athens: Govostis, 1940); *Palia Mazurka se
rythmo vrohis* (Athens: Govostis, 1943); *Dokimasia* (Athens: Govostis, 1943); *O syntrofos*
(Athens: Govostis, 1945); *A anthropos me to garyfallo* (Bucharest: Ekdotiko Nea Ellada, 1952);
Agrypnia (Athens: Pyxida, 1954); *Proino astro* (Athens, 1955); *He sonata tou selenofotos* (Athens:

143

Kedros, 1956); *Chroniko* (Athens: Kedros, 1957); *Hydria* (Athens: 1957); *Apoheretismos* (Athens: Kedros, 1957); *Cheimerine diavgeia* (Athens: Kedros, 1957); *Petrinos Chronos* (Burcharest: Politikes Ke Logotechnikes Ekdoseis, 1957); *Otan erchetai ho xenox* (Athens: Kedros, 1958); *Any potachti Politeia* (Bucharest: Politikes Ke Logotechnikes Ekdoseis, 1958); *He architectoniki ton dentron* (Bucharest: Politikes Ke Logotechnikes Ekdoseis, 1958); *Hoi gerontisses k 'he thalassa* (Athens: Kedros, 1959); *To parathyro* (Athens: Kedros, 1960); *He gefyra* (Athens: Kedros, 1960); *Ho mavros Hagios* (Athens: Kedros, 1961); *Poiemata [4 vols]* (Athens: Kedros, 1961-75); *To nekro spiti* (Athens: Kedros, 1962); *Kato ap'ton iskio tou vounou* (Athens: Kedros, 1962); *To dentro tis fylakis kai he gynaikes* (Athens: Kedros, 1963); *Martyries [2 vols]* (Athens: Kedros, 1963-66); *Dodeka poiemata gia ton Kavafe* (Athens: Kedros, 1963); *Paichnidia t'ouranou kai tou nerou* (Athens: Kedros, 1964); *Philoctetes* (Athens: Kedros, 1965); *Orestes* (Athens: Kedros, 1966); *Ostrava* (Athens: Kedros, 1967); *Petres, Epanalepseis, Kinglidoma* (Athens: Kedros, 1972); *He epistrofe tes Iphigeneias* (Athens: Kedros, 1972); *He Helene* (Athens: Kedros, 1972); *Cheironomies* (Athens: Kedros, 1972); *Tetarte diastase* (Athens: Kedros, 1972); *Chrysothemis* (Athens: Kedros, 1972); *Ismene* (Athens: Kedros, 1972); *Dekaochto lianotragouda tes pikres patridas* (Athens: Kedros, 1973); *Diadromos kai skala* (Athens: Kedros, 1973); *Graganda* (Athens: Kedros, 1973); *Ho afanismos tis milos* (Athens: Kedros, 1974); *Hymnos kai threnos gia tin Kypro* (Athens: Kedros, 1974); *Kapnismeno tsoukali* (Athens: Kedros, 1974); *Kodonostasio* (Athens: Kedros, 1974); *Ho tikhos mesa ston kathrefti [The Wall in the Mirror]* (Athens: Kedros, 1974); *Chartina* (Athens: Kedros, 1974); *He Kyra ton Ambelion* (Athens: Kedros, 1975); *Ta Epikairika 1945-1969* (Athens: Kedros, 1975); *He teleftea pro Anthropou Hekatontaetia* (Athens: Kedros, 1975); *Hemerologhia exorias* (Athens: Kedros, 1975); *To hysterografo tis doxas* (Athens: Kedros, 1975); *Mantatoforos* (Athens: Kedros, 1975); *To thyroreio* (Athens: Kedros, 1976); *To makrino* (Athens: Kedros, 1977); *Gignesthai* (Athens: Kedros, 1977); *Epitome [selection of poems]* (Athens: Kedros, 1977); *Loipon?* (Athens: Kedros, 1978); *Volidoskopos* (Athens: Kedros, 1978); *Toichokolletes* (Athens: Kedros, 1978); *To soma kai to haima* (Athens: Kedros, 1978); *Trochonomos* (Athens: Kedros, 1978); *He pyle* (Athens: Kedros, 1978); *Monemavassiotisses* (Athens: Kedros, 1978); *To teratodes aristourhima* (Athens: Kedros, 1978); *Phaedra* (Athens: Kedros, 1978; *To roptro* (Athens: Kedros, 1978); *Mia pygolampida fotizei ti nychta* (Athens: Kedros, 1978); *Grafe tyflou* (Athens: Kedros, 1979); *'Oneiro kalokerinou messimeriou* (Athens: Kedros, 1980); *Diafaneia* (Athens: Kedros, 1980); *Monochorda* (Athens: Kedros, 1980); *Ta erotica* (Athens: Kedros, 1981); *Syntrofica tragoudia* (Athens: Synchroni Epochi, 1981); *Hypokofa* (Athens: Kedros, 1982); *Italiko triptycho* (Athens: Kedros, 1982); *Moyovassia* (Athens: Kedros, 1982); *To choriko ton sfougarhadon* (Athens: Kedros, 1983); *Teiresias* (Athens: Kedros, 1983); *Arga, poli argá mésa sti nihta* (Athens: Eri Ritsou and Kedros, 1991).

ENGLISH LANGUAGE TRANSLATIONS:

Romiossini: The Story of the Greeks (Paradise, California: Dustbooks, 1969); *Poems,* trans. by Alan Page (Oxford: Oxonian Press, 1969); *Romiossini and Other Poems* (Madison, Wisconsin: Quixote Press, 1969); *Gestures and Other Poems* 1968-1970, trans. by Nikos Stangos (London: Cape Goliard Press/New York: Grossman, 1971); *Contradictions,* trans. by John Stathatos

(Rushden, Northamptonshire: Sceptre Press, 1973); *Selected Poems*, trans. by Nikos Stangos (Harmondsworth, England: Penguin, 1974); *Eighteen Short Songs of the Bitter Motherland*, trans. by Amy Mims (St. Paul, Minnesota: North Central, 1974); *The Moonlight Sonata*, trans. by John Stathatos (New Maiden, Surrey: Tangent, 1975); *The Corridor and Stairs*, trans. by Nikos Germanacos (Curragh, Ireland: Goldsmith Press, 1976); *The Fourth Dimension: Selected Poems*, trans. by Rae Dalven (Boston: Godine, 1976); *Chronicle of Exile*, trans. by Minas Savvas (San Francisco: Wire Press, 1977); *Ritsos in Parenthesis*, trans. by Kimon Friar (Princeton, New Jersey: Princeton University Press, 1979); *Scripture of the Blind*, trans. by Kimon Friar and Kostas Myrsiades (Columbus: Ohio State University Press, 1979); *Subterranean Horses*, trans. by Minas Savvas (Columbus: Ohio State University Press, 1980); *The Lady of the Vineyards*, trans. by Apostolos N. Athanassakis (New York: Pella, 1981); *Erotica: Small Suite in Red Major, Naked Body, Carnal Word*, trans. by Kimon Frair (Old Chatham, New York: Sachem Press, 1982); *Selected Poems*, trans. by Edmund Keeley (New York: Ecco Press, 1983); *The House Vacated*, trans. by Minas Savvas (La Jolla, California: Parentheses Writing Series, 1989); *Selected Poems 1938-1988*, edited and trans. by Kimon Friar and Kostas Myrsiades (Brockport, New York: BOA Editions, 1989); *The Fourth Dimension*, trans. by Peter Green and Beverly Bardsley (Princeton, New Jersey: Princeton University Press, 1993); *Late Into the Night: The Last Poems of Yannis Ritsos*, trans. by Martin McKinsey (Oberlin, Ohio: Oberlin College Press/Field Translation Series, 1995)

A Small Invitation

Come to the luminous beaches—he murmured to himself
here where the colors are celebrating—look—
here where the royal family never once passed
with its closed carriages and its official envoys.

Come, it won't do for you to be seen—he used to say—
I am the deserter from the night
I am the breacher of darkness
and my shirt and pockets are crammed with sun.

Come—it's burning my hands and my chest.
Come, let me give it to you.

And I have something to tell you
which not even I must hear.

Athens, 1938

    —Translated from the Greek by Kimon Friar

from Romiossini

VI

Thus with the sun breasting the sea that whitewashes the opposite
   shore of day,
the latching and pangs of thirst are reckoned twice and three times over,
the world wound is reckoned from the beginning,
and the heart is roasted dry by the heat like Cytherian onions left by
   the door.

As time passes, their hands begin to resemble the earth more,
as time goes by, their eyes resemble the sky more and more.

The oil jar has emptied. A few lees on the bottom. And the dead mouse.
The mother's courage has emptied together with the clay pitcher and
   the cistern.
The gums of the wilderness are acrid with gunpowder.

Where can oil be found now for St. Barbara's oil-wick,
where is there mint now to incense the golden icon of the twilight,
where is there a bit of bread for the night-beggar to play her
      star-couplets for you on her lyre?

In the upper fortress of the island the barbery figs and the asphodels
      have grown rank.
The earth is ploughed up by cannon fire and graves.
The bombed-out Headquarters gapes, patched by sky. There is not the
      slightest room
for more dead. There is no room for sorrow to stand in and braid her hair.

Burnt houses that with eyes gouged out scan the enmarbled sea
and bullets wedged in the walls
like knives in the ribcage of the saint tied to a cypress tree.

All day long the dead bask on their backs in the sun,
and only when night falls do soldiers drag themselves on their bellies
      over smoked stones,
and with their nostrils search for the air beyond death,
search for the shoes of the moon as they chew a piece of bootleather,
strike at a rock with their fists in hopes a knot of water will flow,
but the wall is hollow on the other side
and once again they hear the shell twisting and turning as it strikes
      and falls into the sea
and once again they hear the screams of the wounded before the gate.

Where can one go now? Your brother is calling you.
The night is built everywhere with the shadows of alien ships.
The streets are barricaded with rafters.
There are ways open only for the high mountains.
And they curse the ships and bite their tongues
to hear their pain that as yet has not turned to bone.

On the parapets the slain captains stand guard at the fortress;
their flesh is melting away under their clothing. Eh, brother, haven't
      you tired?
The bullet in your heart has budded,
five hyacinths have poked out their heads in the armpit of the day
      rock
breath by breath the musk-fragrance tells you the legend—don't you
      remember?

tooth by tooth the wound speaks to you of life,
the cammomile planted in the filth of your large toe
speaks to you of the beauty of the world.

You take hold of the land. It is yours. Damp with brine.
Yours is the sea. When you uproot a hair from the head of silence
the fig tree drips with bitter milk. Wherever you may be, the sun sees you.

The Evening Star twists your soul in its fingers like a cigarette,
as it is, you smoke your soul lying on your back.
wetting your left hand in the starlight,
your gun glued to your right hand like your betrothed
to remember that the sun has never forgotten you
when you take out your old letter from your inner pocket
as you unfold the moon with your burned fingers you will read of
   gallantry and glory.

Then you will climb to the highest outpost of your island
and using the star as a percussion cap, you will fire in the air
above the walls and the masts
above the mountains that stoop like wounded infantrymen
only that you may boo at ghosts until they scurry under the blanket's
   shadow.

You will fire a shot into the bosom of the sky to find the azure mark
somewhat as though you were trying the find the ripple of a woman
somewhere on her blouse, and who tomorrow will suckle your child,
somehow as though you were finding, after many years, the knob on the
   outer door of your ancestral home.

   —Translated from the Greek by Kimon Friar

Summer Noon at Karlovasi

Melted iron, noon, stone shadows.
Cicadas and cicada. Hammer blows at the blacksmith's.
Veins of water lurking under the stones.
The cupola of the closed church glitters.
Insufficient fullness—he said. And there is no one to speak,
there is no one to hear. The passing of a seagull:

a sudden burst of semen. And immediately after,
that unaccountable, inexplicable repentence. Under the mulberry tree
a very significant thud was heard as the donkey
flipped one of its ears to chase away a fly.

Athens, Dhiminió, Sámos, 1953-1957

> —*Translated from the Greek by Kimon Friar*

The Same Meaning

Experienced words, dense, defined,
indefinite, insistent, simple, mistrustful—
useless memories, pretexts, pretexts,
the stress on modesty—stones supposedly,
dwellings supposedly, weapons supposedly—the handle of the door,
handle of the pitcher, table with a vase,
tidy bed—smoke. Words—
you beat them on air, on wood, on marble,
you beat them on paper—nothing; death.

Knot your tie more tightly. Like that.
Be silent. Wait. Like that. Like that.
Easy, easy, in the narrow niche, there
behind the stairs, flat against the wall.

> —*Translated from the Greek by N. C. Germanacos*

The Stairs

He ascended and descended the stairs. Little by little
the going up and the coming down blurred in his tiredness,
took on the same meaning—no meaning at all—the same point
on a revolving wheel. And he, motionless,
tied to the wheel, with the illusion he was traveling,
feeling the wind combing his hair back,
observing his companions, successfully disguised

as busy sailors, pulling nonexistent oars,
plugging their ears with wax, though the Sirens
had died at least three thousand years before.

January-June, 1970

> —*Translated from the Greek by N. C. Germanacos*

Dangers

The dead nailed to the walls, next to the advertisements
of state bonds; the dead propped on the pavements,
on the wooden platforms of the notables, with flags, with helmets,
cardboard masks.
                 The dead
have nowhere to hide anymore, they can't command
their dry bones (negotiable deaths, boxes
lifted by winches, yellow paper with pins). The dead
are more endangered.
                     And he, prudent, with his umbrella,
walking high on the electric wires, a tightrope walker
above the parade, with a handkerchief tied over his eyes,
as the first raindrops began to fall.
                                   Then the storm burst.
The trumpeters were shouting to the women to wring the flags dry,
but they had locked themselves in the basements and had swallowed
    their keys.

March-October 1971

> —*Translated from the Greek by Andonis Decavalles*

The Uncompromising

Streets, avenues, signs, names, doors,
dust, smoke, a tree, self-interest. It was I
who threw the ring into the plate. Every night the beer pubs
open and close with calculated noise. The windows
are opaque with golden letters. The waiters have gone

to the toilets for a smoke. The other man is tired,
gazes at the floor or the wall, avoids seeing,
avoids showing, avoids naming. Every word
is a betrayal. On the billboard table
the flabby woman is lying naked, hiding
her eaten face in her scant hair
as large flies with cut wings walk on her breasts.

Athens, April 27, 1971

> —*Translated from the Greek by Kimon Friar*

Naked Face

Cut the lemon and let two drops fall into the glass;
look there, the knives beside the fish on the table—
the fish are red, the knives are black.
All with a knife between their teeth or up their sleeves, thrust in
    their boots or their breeches.
The two women have gone crazy, they want to eat the men,
they have large black fingernails, they comb their unwashed hair
high up, high up like towers, from which the five boys
plunge down one by one. Afterward they come down the stairs,
draw water from the well, wash themselves, spread out their thighs,
thrust in pine cones, thrust in stones. And we
nod our heads with a "yes" and a "yes"—we look down
at an ant, a locust, or on the statue of Victory—
pine tree caterpillars saunter on her wings.
The lack of holiness—someone said—is the final, the worst kind of
    knowledge;
it's exactly such knowledge that now remains to be called holy.

Athens, September 30, 1972

> —*Translated from the Greek by Kimon Friar and Kostas Myrsiades*

The Distant

O distant, distant; deep unapproachable; receive always
the silent ones in their absence, in the absence of the others
when the danger from the near ones, from the near itself, burdens
during nights of promise, with many-colored lights in the gardens,
when the half-closed eyes of lions and tigers scintillate
with flashing green omissions in their cages
and the old jester in front of the dark mirror
washes off his painted tears so that he can weep—
O quiet ungrantable, you with the long, damp hand,
quiet invisible, without borrowing and lending, without obligations,
nailing nails on the air, shoring up the world
in that deep inaction where music reigns.

January-February, 1975

  —Translated from the Greek by Edmund Keeley

from Carnal Word

XII

The day is mad. Mad is the house. Mad the bedsheets.
You also are mad; you dance with the white curtain in your arms;
you beat on a saucepan above my papers as on a tambourine;
the poems run through the rooms; the burnt milk smells;
a crystal horse looks out of the window. Wait—I say—
we've forgotten Phymonóis' tripod in the woodcutters' guild hall;
the oracles are turned upside down. We've forgotten yesterday's
  bleeding moon,
the newdug earth. A carriage passes by laden with oleanders.
Your fingernails are rose petals. Do not justify yourself. In you closet
  you have placed
tulle bags filled with lavender. The sun's umbrellas have gone mad,
they've become entangled with the wings of angels. You wave your
  handkerchief;
whom are you greeting? What people are you greeting? — The whole world.
A brown water-turtle has comfortably settled on your knees;
wet seaweed stirs on its sculptured shell. And you dance.

A hoop from a barrel of olden times rolls down the hill,
falls into the stream, tossing off drops that wet your feet,
and also wet your chin. Stop that I may wipe you.
But in your dancing, you do not hear me. Well then, duration
is a whirlwind, life is cyclical, it has no ending. Last night
the horsemen passed by. Naked girls on the horses' rumps;
perhaps this is why the wild geese were screaming in the bellow tower.
   We did not hear them
as the horses' hoofs sank in our sleep. Today before your door
you found a silver horseshoe. You hung it above the lintel. My luck—
   you shout—
my luck—you shout, and dance. Beside you the tall mirror is also dancing,
glittering with a thousand bodies and the statue of Hippólytos crowned with
   poppies.
My parrot has gone—you say as you dance—and no one imitates my voice any
   more; aye, aye—
this voice from within me comes out of the forest of Dodóna.
Clear lakes rise in the air with all their white waterlilies,
with all their underwater vegetation. We cut reeds,
build a golden hut. You clamber up the roof.
I grasp you by the ankles with both hands. You don't come down.
You fly. You fly into the blue. You drag me with you
as I hold you by the ankles. From your shoulder
the large blue towel falls on the water; for a while it floats
and then with wide folds sinks, leaving on the surface
a trembling pentagram. Don't go higher—I shout—. No higher.
   And suddenly
with a mute thump we both land on the mythical bed. And listen—
in the street below strikers are passing by with placards and flags.
Do you hear? We're late. Take the handkerchief you dance with, too.
   Let's go. Thank you, my love.

Athens, February 15-18, 1981

—Translated from the Greek by Kimon Friar

Closing Words

The unhappy girl gnaws at her collar.
So long ago. Our mothers are dead.
A hen cackles in the rubble.
We hand no answers. Later,
we stopped asking. Night was falling,
wind blowing. A straw hat tumbled
out of the stands of the empty Stadium. Below,
    in the river,
waternsakes and turtles roamed at will.
And maybe this would serve as closure
for a story already remote from us, strange.

Karlóvasi, 7-6-87

—Translated from the Greek by Martin McKinsey

Nelly Sachs [Germany]
1891-1970

Nelly Sachs grew up in Berlin, the daughter of a wealthy industrialist. She was educated privately, with emphasis on the arts, and at the age of seventeen, she began to write, producing a neoromantic poetry, work she later rejected. In 1921 she published *Legenden und Erzählungen,* which consisted of legends and tales. Her verse appeared in various German newspapers throughout the mid-1930s. But in that same period, her life was caught up in the tragic events of the German Jews, as she watched friends and family sent to their doom. In 1940, she and her mother escaped to Sweden, through the help of Swedish author Selma Lagerlöf, Prince Eugene of the Swedish Royal Court, and a German friend, Gudrun Harlan Dähnert.

It was while living in Sweden in fear and agitiation that she began again to write. "Writing is my mute outcry; I only wrote because I had to free myself," she observed. Beginning with her verse play, *Eli: Ein Mysterienspiel vom Leiden Israels (Eli: A Mystery Play of the Sufferings of Israel),* written in 1943 and published in 1951, she produced several volumes of powerful poetry, each seeking answers for the horrors of the holocaust and a reconciliation with the past. Her masterworks include *In den Wohnungen des Todes* (written from 1944-45, published in 1947), *Sternverdunkelung* (1949), *Und neimand weiss weiter* (1957), and *Fluch und Verwandlung* (1959). In 1961, upon the occasion of her seventieth birthday, her publisher Suhrkamp collected her poetry under the title *Fahrt ins Stablose* (Journey Into a Dustless Realm). Other collections, *Späte Gedichte* (1965), *Glühende Rätsel* (1965), *Die Suchende* (1966), and *Teile dich Nacht* (1971), followed. In 1966 she shared the Nobel Prize for Literature with Israeli author S. Y. Agnon. She died of cancer in 1970 in Stockholm.

BOOKS OF POETRY:

In den Wohnungendes Todes (Berlin: Aufbau-Verlag, 1947); *Sternverdunkelung* (Amsterdam: Bermann-Fischer/Querido-Verlag; Berlin: Suhrkamp Verlag, 1949); *Und neimand weiss weiter* (Hamburg: Verlag Heinrich Ellermann, 1957); *Flucht und Verwandulung* (Stuttgart: Deutsche Verlags-Anstatt, 1959); *Fahrt ins Staublose* (Frankfurt am Main: Suhrkamp Verlag, 1961); *Glühende Rätsel* (Suhrkamp Verlag/Insel-Verlag, 1965); *Späte Gedichte* (Frankfurt am Main: Suhrkamp Verlag, 1965); *Die Suchende* (Frankfurt am Main: Suhrkamp Verlag, 1966); *Suche nach Lebenden* (Frankfurt am Main: Suhrkamp Verlag, 1971); *Teile dich Nacht* (Frankfurt am Main: Suhrkamp Verlag, 1971).

ENGLISH LANGUAGE TRANSLATIONS:

O the Chimneys (New York: Farrar, Straus and Giroux, 1967); *The Seeker and Other Poems* (New York: Farrar, Straus and Giroux, 1970).

O the night of the weeping children!

O the night of the weeping children!
O the night of the children branded for death!
Sleep may not enter here.
Terrible nursemaids
Have usurped the place of mothers,
Have tautened their tendons with the false death,
Sow it on to the walls and into the beams—
Everywhere it is hatched in the nests of horror.
Instead of mother's milk, panic suckles those little ones.

Yesterday Mother still drew
Sleep toward them like a white moon,
There was the doll with cheeks derouged by kisses
In one arm,
The stuffed pet, already
Brought to life by love,
In the other—
Now blows the wind of dying,
Blows the shifts over the hair
That no one will comb again.

—Translated from the German by Michael Hamburger

(from *In de Wohnungendes Todes,* 1947)

And we who move away

And we who move away
beyond all leaves of the windrose
heavy inheritance into the distance.

Myself here,
where earth is losing its lineaments
the Pole,
death's white dead nettle
falls in the stillness of white leaves

the elk,

peering through blue curtains
between his antlers bears
a sun-egg hatched pale—

Here, where ocean time
camouflages itself with iceberg masks
under the last star's
frozen stigma

here at this place
I expose the coral,
the one that bleeds
with your message.

—Translated from the German by Michael Roloff

(from *Und neimand weiss weiter,* 1957)

Bewitched is half of everything

Bewitched is half of everything.
Downward wanders the light
into obscurities—
no knife unscales the night.

Solace lives far
behind the homesickness scar.
Perhaps
where a different green speaks with tongues
and the seas abandon themselves timelessly.

The enigmas' trail of comets
erupts in death,
glows
when the soul
gropes home along its railing.

True, cows graze in the foreground,
clover is fragrant with honey
and the step buries what angels forgot.

Awakening clangs in the city
but to cross bridges
is only to reach a job.

Milk rattles in cans on the street
for all who imbibe death as their last taste.
The laughing gull above the water
still has a drop of madness
from living-in-the-backwoods.

Melusine,
your landless part
is preserved in our tear.

—*Translated from the German by Michael Roloff*

(from *Und neimand weiss weiter*, 1957)

Night, night

Night, night,
that you may not shatter in fragments
now when the time sinks with the ravenous suns
of martyrdom
in your sea-covered depths—
the moons of death
drag the falling roof of earth
into the congealed blood of your silence.

Night, night,
once you were the bride of mysteries
adorned with lilies of shadow—
In your dark glass sparkled
the mirage of all who yearn
and love had set its morning rose
to blossom before you—
You were once the oracular mouth
of dream painting and mirrored the beyond.

Night, night,
now you are the graveyard
for the terrible shipwreck of a star—
time sinks speechless in you
with its sign:
The falling stone
and the flag of smoke.

—Translated from the German by Ruth and Matthew Mead

(from *Und neimand weiss weiter*, 1957)

O sister

O sister,
where do you pitch your tent?

In the black chicken-run
you call the brood of your madness
and rear them.

The cock's trumpet
crows wounds into the air—

You have fallen from the nest
like a naked bird
passers-by eye
that brazenness.

True to your native land
you sweep the roaring meteors
back and forth with a nightmare broom
before the flaming gates of paradise…

Dynamite of impatience
pushes you out to dance
on the tilted flashes of inspiration.

Your body gapes points of view
you recover the lost
dimensions of the pyramids

Birds
sitting in the braches of your eye
twitter to you the blossoming geometry
of a map of stars.

Night unfolds
a chrysalis of enigmatic moss
in your hand

until you hold the wing-breathing butterfly of morning
quivering—
quivering—
with a cry
you drink its blood.

—Translated from the German by Ruth and Matthew Mead

(from *Sternverdunkelung,* 1959)

Line like

Line like
living hair
drawn
deathnightobscured
from you
to me.

Reined in
outside
I bend
thirstily
to kiss the end of all distances.

Evening
throws the springboard
of night over the redness
lengthens your promontory
and hesitant I place my foot
on the trembling string
of my death already begun.

But such is love—

—Translated from the German by Michael Hamburger

(from *Flucht und Verwandlung,* 1959)

Vainly

Vainly
the epistles burn
in the night of nights
on the pyre of flight
for love winds itself out of its thornbush
flogged in martyrdom
and with its tongue of flames
is beginning to kiss the invisible sky
when vigil casts darknesses on the wall
and the air
trembling with premonition
prays with the noose of the hunter
blowing in with the wind:

Wait
till the letters have come home
from the blazing desert
and been eaten by scared mouths
Wait
till the ghostly geology of love
is torn open
and its millennia
aglow and shining with blessed pointing of fingers
have rediscovered love's word of creation:
there on the paper
that dying sings:

It was
at the beginning
            It was

My beloved
It was—

—Translated from the German by Michael Roloff

(from *Fahrt ins staublose*, 1961)

How many blinkings of eyelashes
when horror came
no eyelid to be lowered
and a heap of time put together
painted over the air's humility

This can be put on paper only
with one eye ripped out—

You painted the signal
red with your blood
warning of destruction
moist on the borders
but still without birth

When suffering settles homeless
it expels superfluity
Tears are orphans—expelled
in one bound we follow
that is flight into the Beyond
of the rootless palm tree of time—

(from *Glühende Rätsel*, 1965)

PERMISSIONS

"O the night of the weeping children!" "And we who move away," "Bewitched is half of every-thing," "Night, night," "O sister," "Line like," "Vainly," and ["How many blinkings of eyelash-es'].
Reprinted from *O The Chimneys* (New York: Farrar, Straus & Giroux, 1967) and *The Seeker and Other Poems* (New York: Farrar, Straus & Giroux, 1970).

Jules Supervielle [b.Uruguay/France]
1884-1960

Jules Supervielle was born into a French-Basque
family living in Uruguay. Orphaned, he was raised
by his uncle, spending his childhood on the pam-
pas, a subject of much of his early poetry. At ten he
was sent to Paris for his education, and there he
attended the Sorbonne for college. For a while
Supervielle served in the French army, but he devel-
oped a heart condition that lasted for the rest of his
life. Except for frequent visits to his home city of
Montevideo and for the period during World War
II, he remained in France throughout the rest of his
life.

Supervielle is known primarily for his personal
and imagistically-rich poetry, beginning with his 1925 volume, *Gravitations* and continuing
through his later volumes including *Le Forçat innocent, Les Amis inconnus, La Fable du Monde,
Oublieuse Mémoire, Naissances* and other books of poetry.

Supervielle was also the author of several works of fiction, *Le voleur d'enfants* (1926; *The
Man Who Stole Children*) being the most noted of them. He also wrote a pantomime for Jean-
Louis Barrault, and scripted nine plays, among which *Bolivar* formed the basis of the Darius
Milhaud opera.

He died in Paris on May 17, 1960.

BOOKS OF POETRY:

Brumes du Passé (no publisher listed, 1901); *Comme des Voiliers* (Collection de la Poétique,
1910); *Les Poèmes de l'Humour Triste* (Paris: A la Belle Edition, 1919); *Poèmes* (Paris: Figuière,
1919); *Débarcadères* (Paris: Aux Editions de la Revue de L'Amérique Latine, 1922); *Gravitations*
(Paris: Editions Gallimard, 1925; revised in 1932); *Oloron-Sainte-Marie* (Marseille: Cahiers du
Sud, 1927); *Saisir* (Paris: Editions Gallimard, 1928); *Le Forçat innocent* (Paris: Editions
Gallimard, 1930); *Les Amis inconnus* (Paris: Editions Gallimard, 1934); *La Fable du Monde*
(Paris: Editions Gallimard, 1938); *Poèmes de la France Malheureuse* (Buenos Aires: Editions
Amis de Letrres Françaises Sur, 1941); *Choix de Poèmes* (Buenos Aires: Editorial Sudamericana,
1944); *1939-1945. Poèmes* (Paris: Editions Gallimard, 1946); *Choix de Poèmes* (Paris: Gallimard,
1947); *A la Nuit* (Neuchâtel, France: Cahiers du Rhône, 1947); *Oublieuse mémoire* (Paris:
Editions Gallimard, 1949); *Naissances* (Paris: Editions Gallimard, 1951); *L'Escalier: Poèmes nou-
veaux* (Paris: Editions Gallimard, 1956); *Le Corps tragique* (Paris: Editions Gallimard, 1959).

ENGLISH LANGUAGE TRANSLATIONS:

Supervielle, trans. by Teo Savory (Santa Barbara, California: Unicorn Press, 1967); *Jules Supervielle: Selected Writings,* trans. by James Kirkup, Denise Levertov, and Kenneth Rexroth (New York: New Directions, 1967); *Selected Poems and Reflections on the Art of Poetry,* trans. by George Bogin (New York: Sun, 1985).

Montevideo

I was born, and through my window
Rattled a frail barouche.

The coachman was making the daylight skip
With the flourish and crack of his sonorous whip.

An archipelago of dark
Floated still on the limpid day.

The walls woke up, the sands did too,
That sleep inside them, out of view.

Part of my soul began to slide
On a beam of blue against the sky.

And another small piece later
Got mixed with a slip of flying paper,

But, stumbling on a pebble,
Kept its pristine fervor well.

The day was counting up its birds
And never got the answer wrong.

The scent of eucalyptus
Spread itself upon the air.

In Uruguay on the Atlantic
The air was so easy and so warm
That the colors of the horizon came
To look into the houses.

It was I who was being born, down to the deepest woods
Where the shoots are late in coming
And even down to undersea where the seaweeds wave
To make the wind believe it can blow down there.

The Earth went on in her ceaseless rolling,
Spreading her atmospheres to greet her children,

And feeling on the wave or the sweet deep water
The heads of swimmers and the feet of divers.

—*Translated from the French by James Kirkup*

(from *Gravitations*, 1925)

Without Walls
to Ramón Gómez de la Serna

The whole sky is stained with ink like the fingers of a child.
Where is the school and the schoolbag?
Hide this hand—it, too, has black stains—
Under the wood of this table.
The faces of forty children share my solitude.
What have I done with the ocean,
In what aerial desert did the flying fish die?
I'm sixteen all over the world and on the high mountains,
I'm sixteen on the rivers and around Notre Dame
And in the classroom at Janson-de-Sailly
Where I see time pass on the dial of my palms.
The noise of my heart prevents me from listening to the teacher.
I'm already afraid of life with its hobnailed shoes
And my fear makes me so ashamed that my glance wanders
Into a distance where remorse can't appear.
The walk of the horses on the asphalt shines in my damp soul
And is reflected upside down interwined with rays.
A fly disappears in the sands of the ceiling,
The Latin around us squats and shows us its leprosy—
I don't dare touch another thing on the black wooden table.
When I lift my eyes to the Orient of the teacher's desk
I see a young girl facing us like beauty itself,
Facing us like pain, like necessity.
A young girl sits there, she makes her heart sparkle
Like a jewel full of fever to distant precious stones.
A cloud of boys is gliding toward her lips
Without ever seeming to get closer.
We glimpse her garter, she lives far from pleasures
And her half-naked leg, uneasy, swings back and forth.

Her bosom is so alone in the world that we tremble that she might be cold,
(Is it my voice which is asking if the windows can be shut?)
She would love to love all the boys in the class,
This young girl who has appeared among us
But knowing that she'll die if the teacher discovers her
She begs us to be discreet so she can live for a moment
And be a pretty girl in the midst of adolescents.
The sea in a corner of the globe counts and recounts its waves
And pretends to have more of them than there are stars in the sky.

    —*Translated from the French by George Bogin*

(from *Gravitations*, 1925)

Whisper in Agony

Don't be shocked,
Close your eyes
Until they turn
Truly to stone.

Leave your heart alone
Even if it stops.
It beats solely for itself
from a secret inclination of its own.

Your hands will spread out
from the frozen block
and your brow will be bare
as a great square between
two occupied armies.

    —*Translated from the French by Douglas Messerli*

(from *Le Forçat innocent*, 1930)

Seize

Seize, seize the apple and the statue and the night
Seize the shadow and the wall and the end of the street

Seize the foot, the neck of the lady in bed
Then open your hands. How many birds released

How many lost birds that turn into the street,
The shadow, the wall, the apple, the statue and the night?

Hands, you will wear yourselves out
At this dangerous game.
You will have to be cut
Off, one day, off at the wrist.

*

This memory we hide in our arms in the midst of the smoke and the shouting,
Like a young woman rescued from the flames,
Will have to be laid in the white bed of remembrance, with the curtains drawn,
And carefully considered.
Let no one enter the room!
A great body absolutely naked lies there now
And a mouth that we believed forever dumb
Whispering: "Love," with the very lips of truth.

*

Great eyes within this face, who
Placed you there?
Of what vessel with masts of air
Are you the crew?

Who boarded your decks,
That you must ride
The darkness, open wide?

Black flares on the bulwarks,
Astonished, you complied
With the law of storms and wrecks.

Prisoners of a mirage,
When the strokes of midnight settle,
Lower your lids a little
To give yourself courage.

*

You were moving towards him, woman of the great plains,
A dark binding-together of sun and distance and desire.

And your lips were suddenly seized with frost
When his slow face began to come towards you.

You were speaking, speaking, and ghostly, naked words
Wavered towards him, the words of a statue, numberless.

You made of that man a house of stone,
A featureless façade, unseeing day and night.

May he not let a single window into his walls,
And an open door, that will let him step outside a little?

*

Seize when all else fails me,
And with what hands
May I seize that thought,
And with what hands
Seize, at last, the daylight
By the scruff of the neck,
And hold it wriggling
Like a live hare?
Come, sleep, and help me,
You shall seize for me
What I could not hold,
Sleep, in your larger hands.

*

In the room where I was working a long lizard lay dreaming,
Basking in a sun the sky knew nothing of,

Birds went flashing through the roof as if it was not there.
And I believed myself covered by a mask of secrecy!

New faces, features formed by accident,
Laughed, though without the slightest noise.
The air was natural but without sound,
Everything seemed to be living under one persistent gaze.

As a woman's shoulder began revealing itself,
A man who was emerging from a blank space in the wall
Addressed me, bringing his body nearer than his soul:
"How did you manage to come all this way,

Your face is as naked as a trembling hand.
You need not try to hide your eyes and your knees,
Everyone saw you come in and there is no one like you.
Go away now, for here the light of day disconcerts you.

And there is nothing within these walls that ever thinks of you."

—Translated from the French by James Kirkup

(from *Le Forçat innocent*, 1930)

Beautiful Monster of the Night

"Beautiful monster of the night, palpitating gloom
You display a wet snout from outer space
You approach, give me your paw
And pull it back as if seized with doubt.
I am a friend of your dark gestures, nonetheless,
My eyes plumb the depths of your impenetrable coat.
Can't you see me as a brother of the dark
In this world living like ordinary folk, but of the next,
My purest song kept to myself.
Go, I also know silence's torment
With a hasty heart, by patience wornout,
Knocking without an answer on death's doors.
But every once in a while death replies
When your heart is so scared it beats against its walls,
And you're from a world where they're afraid to die."

Eye to eye, with little steps in retreat,
The monster withdrew into rash shade,
And the sky, as always, studded itself with stars.

—Translated from the French by Douglas Messerli

(from *La Fable du Monde*, 1938)

Tada Chimako [Japan]
1930-2003

Born in 1930, Tada was inspired in her late teens by the poetry of Hagiwara Sakutarō (see *PIP* anthology, volume 1) and Nishiwaki Junzaburō to write poems. *Hanabi* (Fireworks) was published in 1956, followed by nine collections before the definitive edition of her complete poems in 1994. Her seventh book, *Suien* (Water Spray), published in 1975, is a small collection of tanka. Her eleventh book of poems, *Kawa no hotori ni* (By a River), published in 1998, won the Hanatsubaki prize. Her twelfth book, Nagai Kawa no aru Kuni (A Country Where There Is a Long River) was published in 2000 and received the Yomiuri Literary Prize.

Often described as an "intellectual poet"—a term that Tada has not resisted—she argues for her poetry (particularly in her noted essay "The Mirror of Velasquez") that she attempts to combine the senses of intellect and emotional feeling to create sublime pleasure. "All the elements of poetry function together, each word having a value like a number that shifts with the changes in syntax. Even in a short poem the reader must use his intellect to record the possibilities of its infinite complexity. How does such a complex writing create pleasure? The specific images, situations and structures of the poem satisfy not only the emotions and all senses, but the brain's delicate interconnections…. The pleasure that results can approach a pure bliss that is among the human being's most sublime experience."

Majoring in English in college, Tada is also recognized as a distinguished translator of French writers such as Marguerite Yourcenar *(Mémoires d'Hadrien),* Claude Lévi-Strauss, Georges Charbonnier, Antonin Artaud, and Saint-John Perse (see *PIP* anthology, volume 2).

BOOKS OF POETRY:

Hanabi (Tokoyo: Shoshi Yureka, 1956); *Tōgokō* (Toyko: Coliseum, 1960); *Bara Uchō* (Toyko: Shōrinsha, 1964); *Kagami no Machi aruiwa Me no Mori* (Toyko: Shōrinsha, 1968); *Nise no Nendaiki* (Yamanashi: Yamanashi Silk Center, 1971); *Tada Chimako Shishō* (Toyko: Shichōsha, 1972); *Shimendō* (Toyko: privately printed, illustrated by Murakami Yoshimasa, 1975); *Suien* (Kobe: Kobe Books, 1975); *Hasu-kui Bito* (Toyko: Shoshi Ringoya, 1980); *Kirei* (Toyko: Chōsekisha, 1983); *Hafuribi* (Toyko: Ozawa Shoten, 1986); *Teihon Tada Chimako Shishō* (Toyko: Sunagoya Shobō, 1994); *Kawa no hotori ni* (Toyko: Shoshi Yamada, 1998); *Nagai Kawa no aru Kuni* (Toyko: Shoshi Yamada, 2000).

ENGLISH LANGUAGE TRANSLATIONS:

Moonstone Woman: Selected Poems and Prose, trans. by Robert Brady, Odagawa Kazuko and Kerstin Vidaeus (Rochester Michigan: Katydid Books, 1990)

Breeze

Like a loquat stone that rolls on the tongue
smoothly June passes by.
When both the piece of ice put on her palm
and the sorrow congealed in the morning
melt by themselves in the body warmth
she at evening clothes herself in a faint light sky
and alone, idly, gently,
caresses for a time the breeze in her hair.

—Translated from the Japanese by Hiroaki Sato

(from *Hanabi*, 1956)

Convergence

The rain washes away the remaining summer,
in the garden a soaked dripping autumn crouches.

My tongue, cold as a clam,
imprisons soft words
in its shell grown used to the tides.

I put a wet stone reflecting my eyes
on a thinly spread palm,

and my long gaze in the end returns to itself,
abandoning a memory
that lists and sinks like a wrecked ship in the distance.

—Translated from the Japanese by Hiroaki Sato

(from *Hanabi*, 1956)

The Withered Field

Tree-searing winds write and thrash.
The mind no one inhabits
has no horizon.
It's simply, unimaginably, wide.
In the shoes are the feet.
How distant the feet are!
Pushing aside the sun reeling from hunger,
today too, teeth exposed to the wind, I go through the winter field.

—Translated from the Japanese by Hiroaki Sato

(from *Hanabi*, 1956)

Execution

Slowly, slowly, the man inhales the air,
his thick chest swells,
his thick arms rise,
his glistening ax lifts,
into the blue sky,
into the blue sky where birds fly,
his glistening ax rises.

Under his feet is a tiny head,
a thin neck, a torso, and legs;
taking aim, the ax stays still,
in the blue sky where birds fly, it stays still;
the whole world falls silent, that moment,
behold, the white neck begins to stretch, sliding,
under the raised ax,
escaping far off from the bound torso,
the white neck stretches, sliding, endlessly.

—Translated from the Japanese by Hiroaki Sato

(from *Tōgijō*, 1960)

Morning Fireworks

A rose morning,
chewing stale gum,
I walked by the sea.

On the sand a disfigured rock statue blocked my way.
An infant hermit crab
was scratching its cracked heel.

From between my gripped fingers
the sands leaked sandy dreams and lost themselves.
A discarded urn, mouth open,
persisted in drinking the wind that was too dry.

In the offing the islands were dots
unrelated to one another.
From time to time, just about when I'd forgotten them,
snow-white fireworks rose and burst.

—*Translated from the Japanese by Hiroaki Sato*

(from *Tōgijō*, 1960)

Legend of the Snow

And finally the snow began to fall
after the rain, wind, and sand

Stopping the hands of all clocks
the snow slowly went on piling
on the steeples of evil intent
on the castle walls of foul distrust
on the ruts of the wheels that struggled with black mud

Enveloped in the snow cocoon
the town became a legend
became a white pumice gravestone
with countless holes bored in it by the souls, the noctilucae....
(however ill and emaciated, old people
all become beautiful before dying)

Where was reconciliation?
The human town forgot weight
and precariously trembling as a single flower
atop a thin stalk
kept opening one white petal after another
(like a deep gentle wound
that turned into a holy theater)

Where was prayer?
The snow that began to fall at last
after the wind, rain, and sand
laid a white day upon a white night
and never ceased.

—*Translated from the Japanese by Hiroaki Sato*

(from *Tōgijō*, 1960)

The Mirror

The mirror is always slightly taller than I am
laughs slightly after I do.
I blush red like a crab
and cut with scissors those parts of me protruding out of it.

*

I bring my lips close to the mirror and it clouds
and I vanish behind my own sigh
just as for example an aristocrat vanishes behind his crest,
just as a hoodlum vanishes behind his tattoo.

*

This mirror, a graveyard of smiles, traveler,
go to Lacadaemon and tell this:

that, heavily made up, a grave painted white,
only a wind blows through the mirror.

—Translated from the Japanese by Hiroaki Sato

(from *Kagami no Machi aruiwa Me no Mori*, 1968)

Poetry Calendar

I who wait for me
I who do not appear
Today, too, I turned a sheet of ocean
And threw away a clam that died, mouth closed

    The day that can't break   a white beach
    A mother's womb that doesn't give birth   a broken oar

I who wait for me
I who do not appear
Today, too, I turned a sheet of horizon
And threw away a snake slough that's too light

    The day that can't break   a useless parasol
    A suspicious laugh   cold fries

I who wait for me
I who do not appear
Today, too, I turned a sheet of sky
Swept together sooty stardust and threw it away

    The day that can't break   tearful grass
    I turn   I turn
    But I do not appear
    I wait for me
    The world of imaginary numbers   armless love

—Translated from the Japanese by Hiroaki Sato

(from *Nise no Nendaiki*, 1971)

The Autumn Thought

It is, for example, a single eggplant left on a withered branch,
a raw-smelling empty can clunking down a mountain
from its deserted apex toward the bottom of a valley,
the sound of wind that startles the Honorable Toshiyuki[1] studying for tests.
The single paulownia leaf[2] is a worn-out and eternal autumn thought.
Noticing that sound,
even a liar hesitates a little before speaking.

Go, endlessly stepping on the shadow of a slender steel tower
and you come out in the country of a northern tribe far beyond the castle wall.
This rose doesn't put on flowers but has many thorns.
Deteriorating civilization,
Queen of Allergia suffering asthma,
the persimmon on your palm, like the innkeeper,
is tipsy, jolly, and sour at heart.

If you sneak into a room in an alley,
a bachelor acupuncturist stabs a white platinum needle into your nape
and quietly pins you to the wall.
Farewell,
grab the wind fluttering like a sail and leave.
Toward the twilight of Inferno,
today, too, the sun is clunking down like an empty can rusted red.

—Translated from the Japanese by Hiroaki Sato

(from *Nise no Nendaiki,* 1971)

---

[1] Fujiwara no Toshiyuki (died 901 or 907). He is famous for his tanka "Made on the Day Autumn Started": *Aki kinu to me ni wa sayakani mienedomo kaze no oto nizo odorokarenura,* "That autumn has come isn't clearly visible to the eye, yet the sound of wind startles me." It opens the Autumn Section of the *Kohinshū* (no. 169).

[2] A single paulownia leaf falling is a set image in classical Japanese poetry that tells of the arrival of autumn.

Making-up

Facing the mirror I lightly make up
This is what I always do, a custom every night
What isn't a custom
Tonight I become a boy!

A dress shirt and a blazer for a fifteen-year-old boy
Slacks also for a fifteen-year-old boy
These mysteriously fit me right
And I become a boy just before his beard begins to grow

This gamble, it doesn't cost much
Isn't even as risky as a gamble
I may replace a jack with a queen
But it's all right: No one will notice it
(Its rusted hull repainted
Its prow loaded with eyes
The ship launches from orthodox time)

From now on I won't envy any man or woman
Won't need perfumes or two revolvers
If I want to, I can become
A concrete woman
An abstract boy

The night has deepened
Preparations done I'll go now
To someone who's neither husband nor lover
Farewell, strange boy in the mirror
Who's about to become a man, until the daybreak smelling of mother's milk

—*Translated from the Japanese by Hiroaki Sato*

(from *Nise no Nendaiki*, 1971)

Fear of the Kitchen

No matter how peaceful a house may be, it has, by necessity, one room tainted by murderous omens. There, people wield murderous weapons in broad daylight and slaughter pitiable small animals. Those who are already corpses are skinned and cut into pieces—on the sacrificial platform called the cooking board.

The cooking board is purified by blood. You wash the blood off with water and detergent merely to return the sacrificial platform in a state of extraordinary exhilaration to the state of *carte blanche* and make it wait for another purification.

The cook is a priest who sanctifies the corpse to turn it into savoriness in the mouth. His clean white robe signifies his priestly status.

Even a dainty fruit knife acquires, doesn't it, the features of a nakedly murderous weapon when it stabs an apple's red cheek?

That white box which makes a manmade Arctic materialize in a corner of the warm kitchen. A refrigerator or a freezer. It is a space of a different character in the bright, heated kitchen and, like the murderous intent in a tiny corner of the brain of a smiling man, hermetically seals its fatally cold air, along with its darkness, and never lets it out.

The plucked birds and beasts stuffed into this white box—how they resemble the frozen corpses in the morgue!

A room equipped with a number of gas burners where you can freely cook and broil. If you feel like it, you can even turn the knob on and just leave the burner unlit. Your kitchen will soon turn into a perfect gas chamber.

And when you put a whole chicken or turkey on a broiling pan into the oven and close its door, don't you think of the steel door that seals in a cadaver at the crematorium? Even the meager oven in my house can readily broil your baby.

The fury of the water that's put on the fire and made to boil—well, that's hard enough, but how can we wash away its resentment as it's left in the kettle to slowly turn cold?

In the peaceful kitchen, stacked pure-white eggs keep a precarious balance, and a highly sharpened meat knife is suspended above the cook's head like a Damoclean sword.

—*Translated from the Japanese by Hiroaki Sato*

(from *Hasu-kui Bito,* 1980)

Distant Autumn

I sweep together the corpses of cicadas
and bury them in a new hole.
I rise to my feet, wavy pampas grass at eye level;
when I rise further, an azure sea at eye level.

In a distant autumn there was a wedding.
Since then many summers,
many attempts and failures to raise Spanish flies.
One morning a boy swam ashore from the offing,
his hair made of corn silk.
Turning around a fermenting vat,
I persisted in killing centipedes.

All this is painted in ancient murals.
The world is plastered in the walls of caves,
and in time peels away.

Peer into the telescope upside down
and distance the shore of shipwrecks,
the shore where thorns prosper
covering my twenty-year-old body that died by water.
Or perhaps what I am now
is in retreat into the interior of time.
I rise to my feet, an azure sea at eye-level.
I rise further, and from my eyes
scaly clouds magnificently drop away.

—*Translated from the Japanese by Hiroaki Sato*

(from *Hasu-kui Bito*, 1980)

PERMISSIONS

"Breeze," "Convergence," "The Withered Field," "Execution," Morning Fireworks," "Legend of
the Snow," "The Mirror," "Poetry Calendar," "The Autumn Thought," "Making-up," "Fear of
the Kitchen," and "Distant Autumn."
©2003 by Hiroaki Sato. Reprinted by permission of Hiroaki Sato.

Jorge Teillier [Chile]
1935-1996

Teillier was born in southern Chile of French ances-
try, and grew up preparing to be a professor of his-
tory. The writer Teófilo Cid (1914-1964) introduced
him to surrealism, and the student abandoned his-
tory for poetry. Although his father was a militant
communist, Teillier himself preferred to forego ide-
ology in his work, focusing instead on the formal.
However, he sympthazied with the Popular Front,
and his daughter was exiled.

He died on April 23, 1996, just two months short
of his sixtieth birthday. The critic Carlos Olivárez
described him as "unarguably the first poet of the
nation" and spoke of the pilgrimages young poets
would make to the ranch outside of Santiago de Chile, where Teillier spent his last years. His
books of poems include *Para ángeles y gorriones* (For Angels and Sparrows; 1956), *El cielo cae
con las hojas* (The Sky Falls with the Leaves; 1958); *El árbol de la memoria* (The Tree of
Memory; 1961), *Poemas del país de nunca jamás* (1963, From the Country of Nevermore, 1990);
Los trenes de la noche y otros poems (The Trains of Night and Other Poems; 1964), *Poemas
secretos* (Seceret Poems; 1965), *Crónica del forastero* (Foreigner's chronicle; 1968), *Muertes y
maravillas* (Deaths and Marvels; 1971), *Para un pueblo fantasma* (For a Phantom People; 1978),
Cartas para rinas de otras primaveras (Letters for Queens of Other Springtimes; 1985), *El moli-
no y la higuera* (The Mill and the Fig Tree; 1992); and *Hotel Nube* (Hotel Cloud; 1996), as well
as several collections published in Mexico, Peru, and El Salvador.

Teillier's distinctive voice and style are apparent even in his earliest works. Critics have
described how he created a new poetic myth, an emotional language that infused images with
a metarealism or secret realism within subjective time. Teillier's invented world is a place of
silent movies, old songs, books from other countries, foreign places; it is a world viewed with
a nostalgia of mythic dimensions.

BOOKS OF POETRY:

Para ángeles y gorriones (1956); *El cielo cae con las hojas* (1958); *El árbol de la memoria* (1961);
Poemas del país de nunca jamás (1963); *Los trenes de la noche y otros poemas* (1964); *Poemas
secretos* (1965); *Crónica del forastero* (1968); *Muertes y maravillas* (Editorial Universitaria, 1971);
Para un pueblo fantasma (Valparaíso: Ediciones Universitarias de Valparíso, 1978); *Cartas para
reinas de otras primaveras* (Edictiones Manieristas, 1985); *El molino y la higuera* (1992); *Hotel
Nube* (1996).

184

ENGLISH LANGUAGE TRANSLATIONS:

From the Country of Nevermore: Selected Poems of Jorge Teillier, trans. by Mary Crow (Hanover, New Hampshire: Wesleyan University Press/University Press of New England, 1990); *In Order to Talk with the Dead,* trans. by Carolyne Wright (Austin: University of Texas Press, 1993).

Letter of Rain

If you cross the seasons
holding in your hands
the rain of your childhood we should have shared
we will meet again in the place
where dreams run joyously
as sheep freed from the corral
and where the star we were promised
will shine above us.

But now I send you this letter of rain
that a rider of rain carries to you
by roads accustomed to rain.

Pray for me, clock,
in the hours monotonous as the purring of cats.
I have returned to the place
where the ash of ghosts I hate
is born again.
Once I went out to the patio
to tell the rabbits
love had died.
When I am here I shouldn't remember anyone.
When I am here I ought to forget the aromatic trees
because the hand that cut them
now digs a grave.

The pasture has grown too high.
On the roof of the neighboring house
a ball made of rags rots,
left there by a dead child.
Through the poles of the fence
faces I thought I'd forgotten come to look at me.
My friend waits in vain for his lucky star
to flash on the river.

You—as if in my dreams—
come crossing the seasons,
with the rains of childhood
in your cupped hands.
In the winter the fire we light together

will unite us.
Our bodies will make nights warm
as the breath of oxen
and on waking I will see that the bread on the table
has a greater dazzle than enemy planets
when your young hands break it.

> *But now I send you a letter of rain*
> *that a rider of rain carries to you*
> *by roads accustomed to rain.*

> —*Translated from the Spanish by Mary Crow*

(from *Muertes y maravillas*, 1971)

Story of the Afternoon

It is late.
The train to the north has gone by.
In your house supper is getting cold,
skeins fall
from the lap of your sleeping mother.
I have kept still while you talked.
Words are nothing
beside the leaf that comes to life when it passes before your face,
beside the paper boat
you taught me to make.
I have looked only at your reflection in the pool.

It is late.
The hours are skeins falling
from the lap of your sleeping mother.
Let's go back to town.
The frogs uselessly repeat their message.
I'll help you jump a puddle, I'll show you a tramp
lighting a fire in an abandoned shack.
Unreal stars extinguish
the frightened smiles of the red roofs.
Nothing ought to exist.
Nothing but our unmoving reflection
still retained by the pool

and those leaves that sometimes come to life
when they pass before your face.

—Translated from the Spanish by Mary Crow

(from *Muertes y maravillas,* 1971)

Nobody's Died Yet in This House

Nobody's died yet in this house.
The walnut tree's omens
are not yet deciphered
and returning footsteps
are always the ones we know.

Nobody's died yet in this house.
That's what the heavy heads of roses think,
where the do-nothing dew swings
while the worm twists menacingly
in the vineyards' sterile talons.

Nobody's died yet in this house.
No hand seeks an absent hand.
The fire doesn't yet yearn for the one who took care to light it.
Night hasn't collected its powers.

Nobody's died but everybody has.
Unknown faces show up in the mirrors,
others drive our cars to other towns.
I look at an orchard whose fruits I remember.

Only the usual footsteps are heard.
Fire teaches the children its tongue,
dew amuses itself swinging in the roses.
Nobody's died yet in this house.

—Translated from the Spanish by Carolyne Wright

(from *Para un pueblo fantasma,* 1978)

Under the Sky Born after the Rain

Under the sky born after the rain
I listen to a gentle glide of oars in the water,
while I think that happiness
is no more than a gentle glide of oars in the water.
Or perhaps it's no more than a small boat's light,
that light that appears and disappears
on the dark wave-pattern of years
slow as a supper after a burial.

Or the light of a house found behind the hill
when already we believed there was nothing left but to walk and walk.
Or the space of silence
between my voice and the voice of someone
revealing to me the true names of things
by simply naming them: "poplars," "rooftiles."
Distance between the clink of the bell
on the bellwether's neck at daybreak
and the sound of a door closing after a party.
Space between the cry of the bird wounded in the marsh,
and the folded wings of a butterfly
over the crest of the hillock swept by the wind.

That was happiness:
to trace meaningless figures in the frost
knowing they wouldn't last at all,
to cut a pine twig
to write our names for an instant in moist earth,
to trap a thistle plume
to stop the flight of a whole season.

Such was happiness:
brief as the felled acacia's dream,
or the crazy spinster's dance before the broken mirror.
But it doesn't matter that happy times are brief
as the journey of a star unfastened from the sky,
for we can always bring their memories together,
just as the boy punished in the courtyard
finds pebbles to form brilliant armies.
For we can always be in a day not yesterday or tomorrow,
gazing at the sky born after the rain

and listening from a distance
to a gentle glide of oars in the water.

—*Translated from the Spanish by Carolyne Wright*

(from *Para un pueblo fantasma*, 1978)

Story about a Branch of Myrtle

Once upon a time there was a girl
who loved to sleep in the bed of a river.
And she went rambling fearless through the forest
becsuse she carried in her hand
a guardian cricket in a cage.

Waiting for her I changed myself
into the wooden house of her ancestors
high on the shores of a misty lake.
My doors and windows were always open
but the only one who visited us was her cousin Swineherd,
who brought us a gift of lazy cats
which sometimes opened their eyes
so we could see
the processions of country weddings
passing across their pupils.
The priest had died
and every branch of myrtle withered.

We had three daughters
barefoot and silent as belladonna.
Every morning they gathered ferns
and only spoke to us to say
a rider would carry them off
to cities whose names we'd never know.

But they revealed the spells to us
that would teach the bees
we were their masters
and make the mill
give us wheat
without the wind's permission.

We waited for our children,
cruel and fascinating
as falcons on the hunter's fist.

       —Translated from the Spanish by Mary Crow

(from *Cartas de reinas de otras primaveras*, 1985).

Islands of Light Are Swimming on the Grass
in homage to Virginia Woolf

"I should walk among willows or stroll
along the bank of a river where tree tops
touch in the water like lovers." We will walk
by the light of flames
the intimacy of a person's body.

And if I correct what's written, Neville,
the girl will think about Bernard interpreting the writer's role,
Bernard thinks about his biographer (which is true).

"Bernard, the man who carried a notebook in his pocket
to write notes, phrases about the moon."

"Call the waiter. Pay the bill.
We should go
Ought. I should. I detest that word."

I begin to read, bored, that book
but I couldn't stop thinking about you.
But I say: now Rhoda would have written
"Islands of light are swimming on the grass."
It was in the Canyon of the Poor, Beautiful Valley's Mountain.
It was Virginia Woolf devouring rivers with her blue glance.

A love recently arrived
makes me close the book's pages
to write you these poor lines.
Desolate and full of love like the wounds
  one inflicts on best friends.

And the waves will break for you into seas
  where you have never been.
"We have to call the waiter. Pay the bill.
We should go. Ought to. I don't know how much I owe."
  I hate that word.
I leave "The Waves" on the table delivered up
  to scorn or indifference.

And I walk toward something alien waiting for me
with sounds of dominoes and families in debt
who leave to wait for their newly bought cars
and I hear the distant bells of city churches.
A farm worker confuses me with an elementary school teacher
and drives me toward town talking about
the drought, the price of lemons and avocadoes.

I think that I also, like Bernard, have my biographer.
A girl from "The Little Union" Bar who is waiting for my death
  to write a Best-Seller.
The thrushes fly toward the fig trees
and the seagulls keep trailing on by, trailing on by, trailing on by.

Tomorrow I expect to see again "Islands of light
  are swimming on the grass"
in the way that I waited as a child for the Sunday matinee.

—*Translated from the Spanish by Mary Crow*

(from *Hotel Nube*, 1996)

PERMISSIONS

Susana Thénon [Argentina]
1937-1990

Born in 1937, Argentine poet Susana Thénon was
also a translator and artistic photographer. Her
early collections, *Edad sin tregua* (1958), *Habitante
de la nada* (1959), and *De lugares extraños*, con-
tained references to Biblical and classical themes.
Influenced by the Italian I Novissmi poets and by
figures such as the Brazilian poets Carlos
Drummond de Andrade and Manuel Bandeira, as
well as others. Thénon broke with her previous
work in her 1984 collection, *distancias*. In this work
Thénon pushed her spare and terse style further
than previously, and explored a work, as she put it,
in which she "entered a strange zone from which it

would be difficult to return." In 1987 she continued that work in *ova completa,* and in other
works, *Ensayo general* and *papyrus,* incomplete at the time of her 1990 death.

BOOKS OF POETRY:

Edad sin tregua (Buenos Aires: Cooperativa Impresora y Distribuidora, 1958); *Habitante de la
nada* (Buenos Aires: Ediciones Thiriel, 1959); *De lugares extraños* (Buenos Aires: Carmina,
1967); *distancias* (Buenos Aires: Torres Agüero Editor, 1984); *ova completa* (Buenos Aires:
Editorial Sudamericana, 1987); *La morada Imposible* (2001)

ENGLISH LANGUAGE TRANSLATIONS:

distancias / distances, trans. by Renata Treitel (Los Angeles: Sun & Moon Press, 1994)

from *distancias*

1

the wheel has stopped   stop-
two three two three two   the wheel
has stopped   broken inside
only wood   eyes enter
only memory   conic
only memory   face to the sky it is not possible
that she should still burn more should burn still more
burn alone eternal as if the wind   (something)
would not scatter her crumbs her clothes   undone
desired body light of the night   birds
homicides under the bridge   go away cold
(something) in cadence   sea
and it whistled and said   creature mud
said and laughed   trumpet of vein
laughed aimed   trembled flesh
and fired   bundle
        shoes
        flesh
ethereal   (something)
and sun   (a woman)
hatchets of sun   (before the locked door)
scratch the door   (looks for her key) it clears
her chest (says in a loud voice) her eye (open to me i) her hand
(calls calls) the edge (no) of the river (no) of blood
(no) of blood that runs away wild thread black with fear
between threshold and door meeting her steps
the wheel has stopped   stop-
two three two three two   the wheel
has stopped

—*Translated from the Spanish by Renata Treitel*

4

there's a country   (but not mine)
where night is only in the afternoon
(but not ours)
and thus sings a star its free time

throughout death i will think
since dying is not mine
and I still shine with dazzled blood
(there's a country) *the dream of falling*
(there's a country)
and i with myself (and always)
with love unmoved

           —*Translated from the Spanish by Renata Treitel*

6

the great snake that embraces the world
sleeps   you too sleep
i sleep   pure of sound
we smile against the   desperate and alone
among the flowers   no
(you can) no (you cannot)   and of the day
it rains shadow   dawned you tremble with
death   prior to death
i sleep a stranger to the map of the seas   here i read
your dream   no longer here   i read
your wolf-laughter white language   i decipher
no (you cannot no)
and now
the drop falls (drink love)
with a whole sky of packed madness

           —*Translated from the Spanish by Renata Treitel*

12

oedipus

the embrace the embrace in the afternoon
how immortal i have been
and how little the alien future hurts
this stone without rest   you were eternal still
you were the last the first the nothing
and nothing but   sun   your glance my blindness
sun forever yesterday   and we turned night
and the embrace was the sea

—Translated from the Spanish by Renata Treitel

13

the night

i shelter unsheltered
i shelter day blind
delicate flammable
i shelter this old shell
among so many other shells
that bursts with stinking fires
child-gunpowder
and pure reason exalted vertebrates

and the eye grows
ejects fires the hands
and the eye suddenly flesh
goes to meet the unseeing
distills in bars not tears but
iron sharks venereal soup
and the eye of sudden city
gets lost in the museum of wrath
body without funeral
the son rolls like a moon

like that other time
in my creak-filled horror
in my suitcase of bird
the futureless girl
drinks her foolish name

i brood
my light tongue
on this crack
bitter accomplice
of the dayless awakening
i feed on eyelid shine of dead lark

—*Translated from the Spanish by Renata Treitel*

38

and the words

and the
words

and the patios   that burn
long after the sun
no longer crossed by any evil   no
steps embraced

and the patios   and the words

—*Translated from the Spanish by Renata Treitel*

(from *distancias*, 1984)

Stroos

stroos
one of the great evils
that affect wominhood
before they called it stress

and before that strass
or Strauss
it's like a waltz
the shadowless woman stumbled through
there's no drama she's drunk
drunk the bitch

stross

—Translated from the Spanish by Renata Treitel

(from *ova completa,* 1987)

PERMISSIONS

Selections from distancias
Reprinted from *distancias/distances,* trans. by Renata Treitel (Los Angeles: Sun & Moon Press, 1994). Copyright ©1994 by Renata Treitel. Reprinted by permission of Sun & Moon Press.

"Stroos"
©2002 by Renata Treitel. Reprinted by permission of Renata Treitel.

Orhan Veli (Kanik) [Turkey]
1914-1950

One of the original contributors to the *Garip* book, which served as the name—the "Strange—for the generation of Turkish innovators including Meli Cevdet Anday and Oktay Ritay, Orhan Veli came to be one of the leading creators of modern Turkish poetry in the 1940s.

His life was that of a man seemingly living at the edge. A strong drinker, Veli fell into a coma in 1939 after an automobile accident; and a few days before his death in 1950, during one of his binges, he fell into a ditch, and lapsed again into a coma. Many of his poems, moreover, recount his numerous love affairs. But as translator Murat Nemet-Nejat points out, despite the personality of a romantic poet, Veli was in actuality a poet of the ordinary and daily life. Indeed Veli's poetry is often quite simple, but is always imbued with a humor and an underlying spirit of self-irony.

Veli was educated in philosophy at the University of Istanbul, and then worked for the Turkish Post Office and as a literary translator for the Ministry of Education. He also translated numerous French poets into Turkish, including Jules LaForgue and Jacques Prevert. His collected works were published in 1982.

BOOKS OF POETRY:

Garip (Istanbul, 1941); *Vazgeçemedigim* (Istanbul, 1945); *Destan Gibi* (Istanbul, 1946); *Karsi* (Istanbul, 1949); *Bütün Siirler* (Istanbul, 1951); *Bütün Siirler* (Istanbul, 1987)

ENGLISH LANGUAGE TRANSLATIONS:

I am Listening to Istanbul, trans. by Talat Sait Halman (New York, 1971); *I, Orhan Veli,* trans. by Murat Nemet-Nejat (New York: Hanging Loose Press, 1989).

I, Orhan Veli

I, Orhan Veli
The famous author of the poem
"Süleyman Effendi, may he rest in peace,"
Heard that you are curious
About my private life.
Let me tell you:
First I am a man, that is,
I am not a circus animal, or anything like that.
I have a nose, an ear,
Though they are not shapely.
I live in a house,
I have a job.
Neither do I carry a cloud on my head
Nor a stamp of prophecy on my back.
Neither am I modest like King George of England
Nor aristocratic like the recent
Stable keeper of Celal Bayar.
I love spinach.
I am crazy about puffed cheese pastries.
I have no eyes
For material things,
Really not.
Oktay Rifat and Melih Cevdet
Are my best friends,
And I have a lover,
Very respectable.
I can not tell her name.
Let literary critics find it.
I also keep busy with unimportant things,
Only between projects,
How can I say,
Perhaps I have a thousand other habits,
But what is the point of listing them all.
They just resemble these.

—Translated from the Turkish by Murat Nemet-Nejat

Tree

I threw a pebble at the tree.
My pebble didn't fall,
Didn't fall.
The tree ate my pebble,
The tree ate my pebble.
I want my pebble.

—*Translated from the Turkish by Murat Nemet-Nejat*

Edith Almera

Possibly, right now,
He's thinking
Of Edith Almera
By a lake near Brussels.

Edith Almera
Is the first fiddle
In a gypsy orchestra,
Very popular on the nightclub circuit.

Curtsying to
Her applauding admirers,
She smiles.

Nightclubs are beautiful;
A person may fall
In love
With girls playing first fiddle there.

—*Translated from the Turkish by Murat Nemet-Nejat*

Birds Tell Lies

Do not listen, my coat, do not listen
To what the birds are telling you,
You are my confidante in life.

Do not listen, birds tell this lie
With every coming spring;
Do not listen, my coat, do not, ever!

—*Translated from the Turkish by Murat Nemet-Nejat*

Rumors

Who says
I've fallen for Süheylâ?
Who saw me, who
Kissing Eleni
On the sidewalk in the middle of the day?
And they say I took Melâhat
To Alemdar,
Is that so?
I'll tell you about it later,
But whose knee did I squeeze on the streetcar?
Supposedly, I've developed a taste for the fleshpots of Galata.
I drink, get drunk,
Then take myself there.
Forget about all these, guys,
Forget, forget about them.
I know what I'm doing.

And what about me
Supposedly putting Muallâ on a rowboat
And making her sing out loud, "My soul is yearning for you…"
In the middle of the harbor?

—*Translated from the Turkish by Murat Nemet-Nejat*

The Song of Istanbul

In Istanbul, on the Bosphorus,
I am poor Orhan Veli;
I am the son of Veli
With indescribable sadness.
I am sitting by the shore of Rumeli,
I am sitting and singing a song:

"The marble hills of Istanbul,
Landing on my head, oh, landing are the sea gulls;
Hot, homesick tears fill
My eyes,
My Eda,
Full of airs, my Karma,
                 the fountain salt
Of all my tears.

In the middle of Istanbul movie houses,
My mother won't hear of my exile;
Others kiss
And tell
And make love,
              but what's that to me?
My lover,
My fever,
       oh, my bubonic river."

In Istanbul, on the Bosphorus,
I am the stranger Orhan Veli,
The son of Veli
With indescribable sadness.

—*Translated from the Turkish by Murat Nemet-Nejat*

How Beautiful It Is

How beautiful the color of tea
Is
In the morning
In the fresh air.
How beautiful
The fresh air
Is.
How beautiful the young boy
Is.
How beautiful the tea
Is.

—Translated from the Turkish by Murat Nemet-Nejat

Barbara Guest [USA]
1920

Since the appearance of a selection of her poetry in *PIP* no. 2, Barbara Guest has published *Miniatures and Other Poems* (Middletown, Connecticut: Wesleyan University Press, 2002). In 1999 she won the Robert Frost Medal for Distinguished Lifetime Achievement from the Poetry Society of America.

Duda Machado [Brazil]
1944

In the *PIP* anthology no. 3, the books *Zil* and *Cresente* were mistakenly described as magazines. Machado's list of books should read:

Zil (1977); *Cresente* (1990); *Margem de uma ondo* (São Paulo: Editora 34, 1997).

Waly Salomão [Brazil]
1944-2003

Waly Salomão, whose poems were included in the *PIP* anthlogy no. 3, died on May 5, 2003. He was 59 years old. The cause of the death was described as lung cancer.

The New York Times reported Salomão's death accordingly:

Waly Salomão, a Brazilian poet, died here (Rio de Janiero) on Monday (May 5). He was 59.

The cause was cancer.

Mr. Salomão rose to fame largely through his lyrics to songs associated with the tropicalista movement, which combines influences like American rock 'n' roll with traditional Brazilian rhythms. His work can be heard in several songs by Caetano Velos, one of the movement's founders, and in recent years he wrote lyrics for a new generation of artists.

He published his first book of poetry in 1971; its title, *Me Segura que Eu Vou Dar um Troço* translates loosely as "Hold Me Back, I'm Going to Throw a Fit."

Earlier this year, Mr. Salomão was named Brazil's secretary of books by Gilberto Gil, the pop star who is now the country's minister of culture.

INDEX OF VOLUMES 1-4

GREEN INTEGER
Pataphysics and Pedantry

Douglas Messerli, *Publisher*

Essays, Manifestos, Statements, Speeches, Maxims,
Epistles, Diaristic Notes, Narratives, Natural Histories,
Poems, Plays, Performances, Ramblings, Revelations
and all such ephemera as may appear necessary
to bring society into a slight tremolo of confusion
and fright at least.

*

Green Integer Books